Youth of the year! Celestial spring!
  Again descend thy silent showers;
New loves, new pleasures dost thou bring,
  And earth again looks gay with flowers.

The image you see above was the illustration from the April, 1920 *Inspiration* newsletter that was published by the Woman's Institute of Domestic Arts and Sciences which inspired my book *Vintage Notions*. The snippet of poetry was written by Thomas Love Peacock. For a more modern look, I chose to update this edition with the cover artwork from the May 1929 issue of Woman's Institute *Fashion Service* magazine.

Springtime's Challenge

BY THE EDITOR

AT LAST Old Sol has crossed the vernal equinox and spring, delightful spring is here. To most of us the past winter with its unusual abundance of snow and ice has been a trying one. It seemed to be without end. But now that the balmy days have arrived, we shall soon forget our recent hardships and rejoice in the awakening of nature.

And with our rejoicing there will come to us the desire to accomplish more the feeling that we should really assist nature in performing its miracle of changing dismalness to brightness and gladness. This, at least, is what should happen, for springtime flaunts before us a challenge to arouse ourselves from our lethargy and, like her, bring into action the powers we possess for self-improvement.

TO HELP us meet this challenge of springtime— and who can afford not to?—there is within each one of us the ability to forget past trials and hardships and to accustom ourselves to conditions as they are.

"I often wonder," says a prominent writer of today, "why we do not take and use this particular fact to comfort us in our griefs and losses. There are sorrows which at first crush us with a sense of inability to bear them. There are disappointments so keen and chilling as to make us despair of recovering from their shock. And burdens a plenty which so weigh us down that we wonder how we can walk on. 'This, too, shall pass,' says Nature in her changing round of seasons. 'Sorrow, loss, and disappointment are only change. However much we feel we cannot accommodate ourselves to them, nearly always light shines again through darkness, strength that is needed comes, and the way that seemed blocked is open to us.'"

"Off with the old and on with the new," is the motto of those whose achievements are greatest. With springtime, we surely can forget the past and rejoice, for Nature herself sets an example that we cannot afford to ignore.

ANOTHER thing in our favor, if we would answer springtime's challenge, is that there is within each one of us the desire and the ability to do. And nothing arouses our spirit of action so much as a real incentive. Spring, with her loveliness, is of course a stimulus to most of us to key ourselves up to greater effort. Still a day does not pass but that other incentives present themselves. Always there are changes, and these changes must be met. And how satisfactory it is to know that we can meet them. When we compare our efforts of a few years ago with those we are making today, we wonder how we could have been satisfied before.

It is true, too, that desire aroused and challenged leads us on to accomplishments greater than we, at some time in the past, believed possible. I know of a woman who was actually unable to keep back success. Beginning in business in a small way, this woman thought she would be satisfied with merely a good living. But with her growing business and the increased care of her family came greater responsibilities. Thus she was challenged. Almost in spite of her wishes, she put forth more earnest efforts and these resulted in the accomplishment of greater deeds than she thought she could possibly perform.

STILL another point to be considered by those who take up the challenge that this glorious time of the year presents is that satisfaction—a genuine reward—is sure to come from achievement.

And who doesn't glory in merited success? When we can see the results that come from earnest endeavor, be our tasks what they may, we have every right to be happy. The saying, "First the thought, then the deed, and then the glory," applies particularly to those who would advance. We must have the desire to do something; then we must earnestly strive to carry on our work to completion; and then, but not until then, will come our reward.

HOW fortunate for those of us who are inclined to lag is the example that comes with this change of season—spring. By overcoming winter's bleakness, she teaches us how to forget; by bedecking herself in splendor, she creates in us the desire to do; by spreading happiness with her miraculous changes, she illustrates to us the reward that comes from putting forth earnest effort.

We would be unfortunate indeed if we passed through an experience and learned nothing from it. So with the arrival of spring, as new life is entering into all things, let us profit by what she is doing, and, in answer to her challenge, let us prove that we, too, can achieve.

Learning to *Appreciate*

By MARY BROOKS PICKEN
Director of Instruction and Principal of
School of Dressmaking and Tailoring

I WAS asked the other day what I thought was most essential to teach children, and instantly I answered, "Appreciation," because true appreciation of the good things of life will keep one forever away from the gross things. To teach a child to appreciate mother, truth, thoughtfulness, and patience is to build character that will make peace for the owner throughout the entire afterwhile.

Appreciation is the key to knowledge, the key to art, to literature, to good work. Without it, beauty is not seen nor understood and perfection is never acquired. The woman who does not appreciate the texture, beauty, and service of a piece of cloth will have the most difficult time in making a beautiful garment out of it. The woman who does not appreciate her home and her responsibilities there will never make hers a happy home.

RECENTLY a government agent talked to me about the necessary things home women should know, explaining what the government, by means of bulletins, is endeavoring to teach so as to awaken interest. As we talked, it seemed to me that the one essential was to cultivate real appreciation of opportunity, to have these women understand their resources, their own power in their own homes—their individual power of keeping health and sunshine.

It may be because I am denied the privilege of much time at home that the thought of it is brighter to me. Perhaps if I had all the crosses that come with each day in the home, I should fail to appreciate the opportunities that are prevalent there and I should see the opportunities not as diamond dollars, but as leaden crosses. But I believe that with the sense of appreciation that I have acquired I should recognize the opportunity that the home actually affords for keeping spirits gay, hearts together, and bodies well nourished. I believe I should practice the little economies that would result in bigger things and set examples that would serve to build character and hold secure that which makes life permanent.

A THOUGHT that seems a very pertinent creed for all of us women comes from Van Dyke: "Believe in yourself, believe in humanity, believe in the success of your undertakings. Fear nothing and no one. Cultivate a sense of appreciation. Love your work, trust and work, keep in touch with today. Teach yourself to be practical and up to date and sensible. You cannot fail."

We women all hurry so rapidly through the days, forgetting how big they are and how many times we could touch hands with real happiness, if we would but appreciate the opportunity.

A few weeks ago I was traveling all day in a Pullman that had practically every seat sold. I was working with papers and writing busily. A razor saleswoman stopped at my chair with, "Oh, dear, making up reports! Say, I'm three days behind on mine." This woman sat down and talked to me. She had traveled far and near, demonstrating and adjusting razors. I cannot begin to tell you how much I actually learned from this woman, but she gave me more food for thought than I have had in a long, long time, and I never appreciated my kind of work more.

LATER, a woman from across the aisle came over and sat with me. She was a quiet, deep-souled person who had lived and thought and who had a delightful sense of appreciation for humor as well as for serious things. She had been a pioneer in the extreme West. She told me of accomplishments out there—of the women, of church and school difficulties, of community sewing classes, of the inability to procure adequate materials, how one magazine traveled the rounds of all the homes, and how recipes were exchanged and bits of sewing and housekeeping knowledge passed on to the neighbors. As this quiet little lady talked, I seemed to see a little indistinct circle forming round her head and I felt definitely happy just to be in her presence.

WHEN she left me I caught myself wondering what I found so charming about her, and then I realized that it was her ability to appreciate life, situations, and opportunities, and to use them all to good effect. She found beauty in the most obscure places, saw good in people, discovered skill in fingers, and evidenced actual delight in every possible service.

LATER, this same little lady cuddled a baby for a good two hours so that the mother might rest, and she administered every possible attention to a train-sick traveler. And that evening, in the diner, I heard her remark to her husband that she was not at all tired and had really enjoyed the day's travel. When we changed trains at Buffalo, she remarked that she was always so happy to get to Buffalo because there was so much beauty in the Falls—eleven whole miles away!

FROM Gifford Pinchot we learn: "The essential things which distinguish one individual from another, which give one man a higher place among his fellows and another a lower, are just two: first of all, perseverance—the ability to keep everlastingly at it; and, secondly, imagination or vision—the ability to see beyond the present moment and to understand that the work at hand reaches beyond the present moment, and so is worth while."

My little lady of the train evidenced that she knew the virtue of perseverance and the value of vision, for her every act, her every word, was for happiness and cheer. She was unselfish, thoughtful in a most intelligent way, and I am sure the brightness of that visit with her will remain with me always, helping me to appreciate my own opportunities for giving out happiness, for helping others, and for learning to be appreciative of the good that surrounds me. To be appreciative—that I am most eager for, because appreciation makes it possible for me to learn, to bring my neighbors closer, and to recognize the good of every day.

WHEN I read letters from you who have so many things to do, I wish I might drop in some morning to help with the dishes and the straightening up, so that we might sit down together and go over the sewing problems and find in our lessons just the things you want to know how to do. I am sure, if this were possible, we could come closer together, for we would have lighted the torch of interest and enthusiasm, both tools for accomplishment, and would, as a result, be much more appreciative of each other's efforts.

Every day in Institute work I am more firmly convinced of the virtue of interest, for it is the highway to appreciation. When we actually learn to appreciate, things become a part of us. Our knowledge is increased, our skill is heightened, and our enthusiasm toward life and our attitude toward people and situations become sincere. Then, and then only, can we help others, and by helping others help ourselves. Emerson says, "Every man takes care that his neighbor shall not cheat him. But a day comes when he begins to care that he does not cheat his neighbor. Then all goes well. He has changed his market-cart into a chariot of the sun."

The *Transparent* Hat

By MARY MAHON
Department of Millinery

THERE is hardly a week that does not bring something new in millinery to delight the heart of the woman who seeks variety in hats. While the highly vivid tones have found favor with the average American woman, horsehair and transparent maline hats in black, brown, and navy are at present making an equal demand for her attention. These hats are made in almost every conceivable shape and size, and some consist of a combination of Chantilly lace and the popular fabrics of the season. Berton shapes turned up evenly all around and appearing in ever so many unique variations continue to maintain their exalted rank. For their trimming, a row of crushed roses is sewed on the under brim, and, in many cases, a layer of maline is used over the roses to subdue the coloring. Others have the side crown covered with flowers, which, when they show through the upturned, lacy brim, produce an artistic and appealing effect.

THE essential characteristic of the large picture hat is its transparency, and maline is the material that best brings about this effect. Although often considered perishable, it is an undisputed fact that excellent maline will stand a reasonable amount of dampness and hard usage. Then, too, it can be utilized in so many different ways, because it possesses both daintiness and durability, so that, in deft hands, no end of beautiful effects and arrangements can be secured.

SINCE transparency is the result so much desired, the hat shown in the illustration, made entirely of maline on conservative lines, will satisfy those who seek refinement in their hats, and it is a matter of interest that the gradual trend of millinery modes is from the extreme novelty to the more elegant and quiet styles. The striking feature of this hat is its width from side to side. It is made on a wire foundation consisting of two head-size wires, four stay wires, and a steel edge wire. The front and back stay wires measure 3 inches and the side wires 5 inches.

Cut several strips of maline about 2 inches wide and wind the steel edge wire, which is joined with a clip, with these strips until it presents an even, round finish. Then, with the maline folded as it comes on the bolt, or in two thicknesses, double it over the edge wire and, beginning at the back, draw it firmly around the edge. Stretch it as much as possible all the way around and lap it about 4 inches at the back. Secure it firmly with a stitch or a pin, and then draw all the fulness into the head-size, pinning it securely. Next hold the brim over a steaming tea kettle and, while doing so, draw the maline until all the fulness is drawn in at the head-size. Then sew it

with a running stitch around the head-size wire so as to fasten it in place.

FOR the extension tuck, or extra circle of maline, it is necessary to use an extra steel wire about 54 inches long and to join this with a clip to form a circle. Draw the maline around this circle in the same manner as around the frame. After securing the lap at the back, shirr the maline in the

Embroidery and Tissue-Paper Patterns

For the information of many inquiring students, we wish to state that we do not maintain any pattern service other than the plain waist and skirt patterns we send to each dressmaking student with "Tissue Paper Patterns," Parts 1 and 2. However, if any student wishes to obtain a pattern for a design that she has selected from a fashion magazine, and she does not know where to send for it, we shall gladly give her the address of her nearest pattern agency.

A number of the well-known pattern companies furnish books containing illustrations of embroidery designs suitable for practically every purpose and for which patterns can be purchased. Each of the books is well worth the price charged for it.

Following are the addresses of the publishing companies that supply such books for 25 cents; additional charge is made for postage, however.

Butterick, Spring and MacDougal Streets, New York City. (This book includes a coupon good for 10 cents toward the purchase of a pattern.)

Pictorial Review, 216-226 W. 39th Street, New York City.

McCall, 236-350 W. 37th Street, New York City.

Home Pattern Co., 114 Fifth Avenue, New York City.

Embroidery designs are occasionally shown in *LeCostume Royal* and *Fashionable Dress*, but there is no special book illustrating these patterns published.

center with No. 16 cotton thread, catch both ends of the thread securely, draw this string as tight as possible, or until the wire twists, and tie the shirring string firmly. Then steam the maline until all the fulness disappears, making sure that the steam strikes the fulness only, for if it strikes the wire edge it is apt to rust the wire and cause the maline to stick.

Cut the shirring string and remove the wire by first separating the overlap at the back carefully, and then, working the maline back until you can grasp the wire, gently drawing the wire out of the maline circle. Lay this circle on top of the maline brim and join it at the back, allowing it to extend over the edge about 1 inch and fastening it to the edge wire by means of a knot underneath the brim. If desired, two or three maline circles instead of one may be used in the same manner to give a soft, airy touch to the hat.

AN oval-shaped crown is used on this hat, and this can be made of maline or horsehair braid. To give the crown a softer effect, a separate tam of maline is placed over it. This is made by joining a 35-inch strip of maline 9 inches wide to a circle of maline 11 inches in diameter. If you desire a flower trimming, pretty, bright flowers can be appliquéd on the crown and the extra tam of maline sewed over the flowers. If you wish the hat suitable for all seasons in the year, it may be trimmed, as in the picture, with a band of cire ostrich around the base of the crown and a tie of No. 2 moiré ribbon as a finish.

ANOTHER pleasing result can be had in the way of a large transparent hat, which, in reality, is not as large as it appears, by making it on a little solid foundation of pressed netine, a feature that will prove a decided asset because of the protection it affords the eyes when the hat is worn in strong sunlight, a thing heretofore not to be expected in a transparent hat. This foundation measures from 1 to 2 inches in the front and back and about 3 inches on each side, and has a bell-shaped crown. French blue taffeta is used to cover this frame, and 2-inch black horsehair braid is sewed on the extreme edge of the hat, so that it extends out the full 2 inches. The next row is sewed on so that it laps over the first row at least 1 inch, but on the rest of the brim and the crown the horsehair is sewed on plain. The two-tone effect produced by the blue showing through the horsehair is exceptionally good and at the same time somewhat unusual. As a trimming for this hat, a garland of roses, whose long stems twist around the crown, trails from the brim to the shoulder. In this pleasing arrangement of every leaf, thorn, and bud, perfect rhythm is expressed.

The *Utility* of a Separate Skirt

By ALWILDA FELLOWS
Department of Dressmaking

LIMITED means and variety in one's wearing apparel have never been on the most intimate terms. And this season, because of the apparently exorbitant charges made for even ordinary garments, one might expect complete estrangement of these two factors.

Such expectation need not be fully realized, however, for the woman who is not overly stout and to whom a separate skirt would prove becoming may include one or two such skirts in her wardrobe, and by using ingenuity in the selection of other wearing apparel, prepare for practically any occasion that may arise. By this I mean that with the separate skirt one has the basis for many costumes, for this season has ushered in a popularity for separate skirts, the like of which has not existed in some time.

ONE naturally considers the blouse as a natural skirt companion, and as such variety is offered in this particular garment, costumes for different occasions may be afforded by merely a change in the blouse style, provided, of course, that the skirt is a medium type—one not too decidedly tailored and yet not overelaborate in regard to material or design.

For wear under a Polo, leather, or sports coat or with a sweater, nothing has quite the dash and the appearance of fitness that are characteristic of the separate skirt made of plaid wool or silk. This same skirt may be worn with a jacket of plain color to form a suit style that is now very prominent.

"SKIRT talk" naturally reverts to plaids, regardless of the angle from which it is started, for plaids undoubtedly are the center of attention and are developed in such a variety of styles that their vogue is bound to be long-lived. If you are of slender or medium build, you will find a plaid skirt a happy experiment that fits into all the odd times when what to wear is a question. But if you cannot be classed with either of these types, use all your will power to resist the purchase of plaids, for they will serve only to accentuate your build, and, instead, resolve to enjoy the vogue for plaids at a distance.

The tendency of plaid skirts—in fact, of all separate skirts—is to follow long, slim lines, even though a great many of them are knife- or accordion-plaited. The skirts that are not plaited are draped or simply gathered at the waist line and occasionally adorned with little elegancies and decorative details, charming and out of the ordinary because of their having been, in the past, confined only to blouses and dresses.

Loops made of self-material, braiding, odd pockets, pearl buttons, picoted and double-faced ribbons, and flutings, all do their share toward making the separate skirt a very pleasing asset to a wardrobe.

SOME fairy weaver must have had a hand in the creation of the beautiful silks that are being offered this season. In knitted weaves and in ribbed, crêpe, and satiny finishes, one finds silks that are the epitome of all that is lovely for feminine needs and desires. These have been introduced with odd trade names and are shown along with improved and newly beautified weaves of Dew-kist, Fan-ta-si, and Kumsi-kumsa, which are now well known. Other silk materials employed for skirts for sports wear or for festive occasions are tricolette, taffeta, crêpe de Chine, Georgette crêpe, satin, and faille. Such lovely colors as canary, goldenrod, sunset, raspberry, flame, cherry, hydrangea, and turquoise are found in these fabrics.

Woolen materials include Poiret twill, duvetyn, tricotine, tweed, serge, velour, and flannel. Forest shades of brown, green, and blue and black-and-white combinations are prominent in woolens.

STYLE selection is by no means the least important item in the development of a skirt. After you have decided on the material best suited for your purpose and to your type, give deliberate consideration to the choice of a design. The styles shown on this page may help you, for they are not in the least extreme, and with minor changes may be followed for almost all types.

The style at the left may have for its main portion just one straight piece of material that measures several inches more than do the hips. The seam at the center back may be finished in a tuck and accentuated its entire length with buttons.

In order to insert a straight section for knife plaits, slash the skirt at each side back to the hip point and then straight across to the side front. Join a straight section to each of the portions below the hip slashes, making the width of these sections about 2 inches greater than twice the length of the hip slash. Knife plaits require three times as much material as the length into which they are folded; hence the necessity of making allowance for seams on the inserted portion, which, combined with the section left below the hip slash in the skirt, provides the proper amount for plaits. The applied section at each side will cover the joining of the plaits to the hip slashes.

A PLEASING use of plaids is shown in the center illustration. This skirt, also, may be made of straight pieces of material wide enough to give a little "ease" through the hips, and box plaits inserted at each side front and side back to give more width at the lower edge.

If you are inclined to be stout, you will, of course, wish to avoid plaids; but this style developed in plain wool or silk would indeed be an excellent one, for the lines are long and suggestive of slenderness.

BLACK satin as a skirt material has been favored so long that it is almost a standard for this purpose. And what is lovelier than a black-satin skirt, especially one that is oddly draped in a becoming manner? Suggestive of this very material is the *Royal* style shown at the right, but it might also be attractively developed in silk of another kind.

At the first glance you may consider the development of this design very difficult, but if you will attempt a little experimental work by draping a straight piece of material on a dress form, you will be surprised at the ease with which the style may be evolved.

In draping, first pin the end of the material at the left side, a little toward the back. Bring the material straight across the front and then across the back, gathering in the fulness at the waist line. Then, at the left side front, draw the material up toward the waist line and with a little adjustment it will form the draped, or distended, effect at the side.

The girdle, if made of bias material, will drape in very softly at the waist line. A touch of contrast may be introduced by piping it at the lower edge with a color.

Cakes and Cookies *a Plenty*

WHEN eggs become more plentiful and consequently drop in price, we immediately have visions of all kinds of delicious cakes that we have refrained from making because of the economical habits we have recently developed. All during the winter, we find ourselves making such statements as, "I want so much to make an extra fine cake for my party, but eggs are so high in price that I feel as if it would be an extravagance to use so many."

So what delights we experience when we realize that we are at last justified in making a feathery sunshine cake for over the week-end, that we can surprise father with a huge piece of his favorite chocolate cake—the melt-in-your-mouth kind—and that we can satisfy little brother and sister so far as cookies are concerned; in fact, that we can, for a little while at least, indulge both our cooking fancies and our family's appetites with these dainty foods.

TO MAKE cake successfully—and this is one of the ambitions of the modern housewife—there are a few principles that should be faithfully observed. In the first place, all the utensils and ingredients should be collected and conveniently placed before the actual mixing of the cake is begun. In addition, any of the ingredients that require preparation, such as fruits and nuts, should receive it. Care should also be used to measure accurately, for much of the success of a cake depends on the attention that is given to this matter. To insure lightness in the finished cake, the flour should usually be sifted once before it is measured and then again with the baking powder, soda, or cream of tartar. The eggs required should be broken and beaten just before they are added. Finally, when the cake pans have been prepared, the housewife may consider herself ready to combine the ingredients.

NO FORM of sponge cake meets with so much favor as sunshine cake, particularly for social functions and for serving with various frozen desserts, for while it is characterized by daintiness, its absence of butter prevents it from being very rich.

Sunshine Cake

6 eggs	¾ c. flour
⅓ tsp. cream of tartar	1 tsp. lemon juice
1 c. sugar	1 tsp. vanilla

Separate the eggs. Beat the yolks with a rotary beater until they are thick and lemon-colored. Beat the egg whites until they are foamy, add the cream of tartar, and continue beating until they are dry. Fold the sugar into the egg whites and then

By LAURA MACFARLANE
Editorial Department

fold the yolks into this mixture. Sift the flour several times and add it. Add the lemon juice and vanilla, pour into a sponge-cake pan, and bake.

IF AN especially good chocolate cake is wanted, the chocolate nut layer cake here given should be tried. A white boiled icing is suggested for filling and covering, but a chocolate icing may be used in case an entire dark cake is preferred.

Chocolate Nut Cake

¼ c. butter	4 tsp. baking powder
1 c. sugar	2 sq. chocolate
1 egg	½ c. chopped nuts
1 c. milk	1 tsp. vanilla
2 c. flour	

Cream the butter, add the sugar gradually, beat the egg, and add it to the mixture. Stir in alternately the milk and the flour and baking powder. Melt the chocolate in a double boiler and stir this into the dough. Fold in the chopped nuts, add the vanilla, and bake in a loaf or in two rather thin layers. When cool, ice the first layer with white boiled icing, place the other layer on this, and cover with the same icing.

FOR the recipe for the famous Lady Baltimore cake, we must go back to the original Lord Baltimore family, who always enhanced the Christmas holidays with cake of this kind. But it is a shame not to make this cake at other times of the year, for it is so well suited to festivities of all kinds at which a delicious cake is desired.

Lady Baltimore Cake

½ c. butter	4 tsp. baking powder
1 c. sugar	3 egg whites
¾ c. milk	1 tsp. vanilla
2 c. flour	

Cream the butter, add the sugar gradually, and continue creaming. Stir in the milk. Sift the flour and baking powder together and add them. Fold in the stiffly beaten egg whites and add the vanilla. Bake in square layer pans or in two thick layers in loaf-cake pans. When cold, spread the following filling between the layers and ice with any desirable white icing.

Filling for Lady Baltimore Cake

2 c. sugar	½ c. figs or dates, chopped
½ c. milk	1 c. chopped nuts
1 c. raisins, chopped	

Cook the sugar and milk until it forms a soft ball when dropped in cold water. Remove from the fire and cool. Beat until it begins to look creamy, and then add the raisins, figs or dates, and nuts. When stiff enough, spread a thick layer on one layer of the cake, place the other layer of cake on top, and cover with a thin layer of white icing.

NOTHING in the way of food can take the place of cookies so far as children are concerned. And for that matter, what grown-up does not beam at the sight of a plate of these little cakes if they are crisp and tasty? The following recipe is a very simple one to follow, but it produces a result that will be disappointing to no one.

If these cookies are made rather small and cut in unusual ways, they may be served with tea at informal afternoon functions. It is possible to procure a variety of cutters for this purpose.

Lemon Cookies

1 c. shortening	1 lemon
2 c. sugar	1 tsp. soda
3 eggs	4 c. flour

Cream the shortening and add the sugar and eggs. Grate the rind of the lemon into the mixture, and stir in the lemon juice to which the soda has been added. Add the flour. Roll as thin as possible and cut in any desired shape.

THERE are times when one's family want a change from layer or loaf cake and still do not find cookies sufficient to meet the needs. Cup or drop cakes should be made at such times, for they seem to fill the gap between these two kinds and at the same time offer an opportunity for variety. Too much cannot be said in favor of Roxbury cakes, for they are a splendid kind of small cakes. The accompanying recipe makes one dozen cakes.

Roxbury Cakes

¼ c. butter	½ tsp. cinnamon
½ c. sugar	½ tsp. ground cloves
2 eggs	1½ tsp. baking powder
½ c. molasses	½ tsp. soda
½ c. milk	¾ c. raisins
1¾ c. flour	½ c. English walnut meats
½ tsp. nutmeg	

Cream the butter and add the sugar gradually. Beat the eggs and add them. Add the molasses and milk. Mix and sift the dry ingredients and stir these into the first mixture. Fold in the finely chopped raisins and nuts. Pour into greased and floured muffin pans, bake in a moderate oven, and ice with white icing.

Sources of Spring Millinery

NOTHING is more distinctive than a stylish little hat made at home. To have a hat admired by one's friends and be able to say "I made it myself," is the delight of nearly every woman. But where to get the inspiration for something different and yet smart is a problem of great moment. This season we can do no better than to turn to the Orient. The toque, or turban, so much in vogue at present, has been worn for generations in the East, where it is possible to find as many combinations as the most fastidious could desire.

REPRESENTATIVES of the Inter-church World Movement, who are making a social and economic survey of the Orient, report that the native of India binds his head in an endless variety of ways. The caste of the wearer is distinguished by the head dress, which is sometimes plain and unadorned and sometimes bejeweled and covered with embroidery. Since climatic conditions in many parts of the East have made it necessary for the head to be covered as a protection from the heat of the sun, Sultans and those of noble birth have devoted particular care to the arrangement of the turban.

Turbans this spring can be draped extensively after the model of the Eastern Sultan. Embroidered material, grass cloth, raffia, and silk duvetyn are excellent for the draped toque. The new shiny black oil-cloth is also popular for the turban, or toque. This may be left plain or embroidered over the entire surface with silken threads in imitation of Oriental decorations. Again, strands of bright-colored raffia can be used to decorate it in spots.

EGYPT, too, offers suggestions for the home milliner. The head dress of Cleopatra is a good model for the latest style in turbans. A close fitting hat, made with as little stiffening as possible over a light frame, unadorned save for the dangles over the ears, is almost a replica of the turban that graced the head of the illustrious Egyptian queen centuries ago. The dangles may be of beads, feathers, tassels, or jet, and should hang over the hair and the ears. These ornaments may vary with the hat. If the toque is soft in lines and general makeup, fancies that stick straight out are very fetching. For this style of trimming, pompons of soft silk or ball-like effects made of aigrettes should be used.

A VARIATION of the outline of the turban may be made by using a shape high in front and extended at either side. A hat of this variety made of tan maline, with buttercups embroidered in regular succession on its surface, would give an impression of a bright spring field and be extremely alluring.

Turbans can also be made of cretonne, organdie, or gingham to match the dress. Straw is among the least popular of materials this season, so there is abundant opportunity to utilize odds and ends for hats. No color is too bright and no shape too unique, provided the proper touch is given.

Woman's Institute *Question-Box*

Want to Get Acquainted?

The following Institute students desire to become acquainted with other Institute students residing in their localities:

Seattle, Wash............................H. L. C.
Urich, Mo...............................M. F. G.
Port Arthur, or Fort William, Ont., Can...J. R. M.
Minneapolis, Minn.......................M. M. G.
Milwaukee, Wis..........................J. J. H.
Montreal, Que., Canada..................C. E. S.
New York City...........................M. U.
Napa, or San Francisco, Calif...........R. W.
Dixon, Mont.............................H. C. M.
Manzanolo, Colo.........................J. G. S.
Vandalia, Ill...........................H. J. H.
East Orange, N. J.......................L. F.
Bellingham, Wash........................B. L. M.
New Haven, Conn.........................V. M.
Plaquemine, La..........................L. M. W.
Windsor Locks, Conn.....................A. C.
Buffalo, N. Y...........................G. McN.
Isabella, Porto Rico....................A. V.
Rosston, Okla.; Shawnee, Okla.; Alva, Okla.;
    Cary, N. C.; Windom, Kans.; Inam, Kans..T. H.
New Orleans, La.........................E. G.
Montpelier, Vt..........................L. B. C.
Minneapolis, Minn.......................W. T. G.
West Haven, Conn........................T. E. C.
Twin Falls, Idaho.......................M. H.
Brooklyn, N. Y..........................J. McD.
Burlington, Vt..........................R. G.

I should like to correspond with an Institute student 19 or 20 years of age, who is taking the Dressmaking Course.
                B. E. B.

I should like to become acquainted with a Woman's Institute student taking the Millinery or Dressmaking Course, residing in Danville, Ill.
                E. V. P.

I should like to hear from some one who wishes to start a millinery or a dressmaking business in a small town in northern Iowa.
                S. S.

I should like to know if there is a Woman's Institute student in Allegan, Mich., or in some other town, who would like to come here to start dressmaking. There is an excellent opening here for some one who has the ability to make distinctive clothes.
                S. R.

I should like to meet or correspond with Woman's Institute students living in Erie, Pa.
                M. R.

If other Woman's Institute students would like to get in touch with the inquiring students, we shall be glad to supply the addresses.

Marking Skirt Length

Isn't there any plan I can follow in marking the correct length for my skirts? I always have a great deal of difficulty in turning an even line around the lower edge, and, as I live in the country, I have no one near to help me.
                M. R. D.

You will find the following method very practical: Stand a yardstick upright on the floor with one end touching your figure. Make a mark on the skirt at the point where the upper end of the yardstick touches it. Then move the yardstick around the figure, placing marks or pins a few inches apart. After the skirt is removed, these marks will serve as a guide in marking the lower edge. Turn the lower edge of the skirt at the center front after the length has been decided on. Remove the skirt and measure down from each mark or pin this same distance. Mark or turn the edge evenly, so that the entire skirt is exactly the same length below the marks at the upper end of the yardstick. You should remember that the difference in the front, side, and back lengths of a skirt exists between the hip line and the waist line, rather than between the hip line and the hem.

For very short figures, it may be necessary to use a stick that is shorter than 36 inches. Any straight stick long enough to reach from the floor up to the fullest part of the hips will serve nicely.

Play Suits for Boys

What materials would you suggest for play suits for a very young boy? I want to obtain fabrics and colors that will withstand frequent washings.
                S. L.

Unbleached muslin of rather loose weave is an excellent material for this purpose. This may be used for little overall styles of various kinds or for entire suits. Suits of this material are almost invariably hand embroidered with yarn in large, attractive designs or in outline or blanket stitches. In this manner, a very lowly material demands unusual respect and admiration.

Medium or dark blue, grayed green, brown, and tan chambray combine utility with smartness in play suits that are smocked or otherwise embroidered.

Rather heavy printed cottons in floral, animal, or bird designs figure prominently in showings of play suits, but most of these are intended for girls. For very ordinary wear, little overalls of khaki or blue denim, trimmed with bright-red pipings are sure to please.

You may be interested in the little play-suit styles that are shown on this page. Fine, striped ginghams are used for two of the models, and striped percale is employed for trimming the style developed in plain color. These are simple, practical styles that can be quickly developed.

Our Students' Own Page

$50 Negligée for Only $14

When you acquire the ability to make your own clothes, the high cost of dressing will take a sudden tumble; and it will be down to stay down, for you will ever after be independent of expensive ready mades or high-priced dressmakers. The savings made by Miss Barbe, one of our Texas members, are not different from those being made by thousands of our members. Wouldn't *you* like to make some savings like these on *your* clothes? Miss Barbe writes:

I have finished my negligée about which I wrote you, and it is perfectly beautiful. Every one who sees it thinks it is wonderful the way I have learned to sew so well, and in such a short time. This negligée would cost at least $50 if bought ready made. The materials cost about $14. I have made seventeen pieces of silk underwear, most of which have some embroidery on them, three silk shirts with embroidered monograms, and two cotton shirts of striped materials.

Good Bread by Our Method

Here is a letter from one of our North Dakota members, Mrs. A. Susie Meriam, who is enrolled for Dressmaking, Millinery, and Cookery; and the letter itself is excellent evidence that she is making excellent progress in at least one of these subjects. Mrs. Meriam writes:

You can imagine how proud my husband is to have me so interested and doing so well. I cannot tell you how many people he has told about the Courses. Another thing that pleases him is the fine bread I can make, using yeast foam. I had always used the compressed cake and had no luck until I had to make bread in my cookery lesson.

Succeeding Under Difficulties

Some time ago we received a letter from one of our members who said she thought we were making a mistake in always publishing letters from women who had been so successful. She thought it was well to tell about some of the difficulties some of our members were having. So we are giving here a letter from one of our members who surely did have some difficulties. But she succeeded in spite of her difficulties. This letter came a short while ago from Miss Thelma Reed, one of our Ohio members, who writes:

I was bedfast when I wrote for the Course and my lessons helped me wonderfully to shorten the long hours of convalescence. Later I was able to go around over the house by the aid of crutches, which I still have to use, and I started to put my millinery knowledge to good use. I have been making hats for the public for over 7 months now, and I clear over $70 a month. Don't you think that is real good for a shut-in?

Savings That Are Worth While

For the woman who has recently been on a shopping tour, the following letter from Miss Ella Quantz, one of our enthusiastic Ontario members, will be very refreshing, especially when she realizes that by the Woman's Institute method only a few weeks will be required to give *her* just such ability as Miss Quantz is turning into such effective savings. Miss Quantz writes:

I feel your Course is of equally as much help to me as my other studies were. Every one in the neighborhood seems to come to me for advice about their clothes. The prices of things in Toronto are beyond all reason. I am just finishing up a simple little dress of silk poplin, the material for which has cost me less than $10. You could not get anything like it in town under at least $65, and I will have a dress distinctly unusual as well as stylish, which is quite a satisfaction.

Designing Very Simple Now

Planning one's clothes becomes a very simple matter once one realizes that all of the many hundreds of designs seen in the stores or fashion magazines are built on just a few foundation patterns. And, as a student of the Institute, you will get a thorough knowledge of how to develop from these few foundation patterns any style or design that may appeal to your fancy. In this connection, you will be interested in the following letter from Miss Pearl C. Hansen, a Minnesota member:

A fashion picture now does not have the horror of designing connected with it as before. I can now see that I would use one foundation or another and develop the new pattern from it. When one knows that there are merely a few foundation patterns and that all patterns hinge on them instead of on the multitude of separate patterns that one thought there were formerly, it is far more interesting to look through books of fashions and by simply changing different lines in the foundation pattern secure the desired effect. I can now see why some faddish and freakish appearing designs have their place and have some clever features about them.

I am interested in trying to fit different materials to different styles to give the most pleasing lines. Some fashions call for heavy fabrics, and some heavy materials could not be used at all for some of the styles exhibited or shown in the magazines. I am interested in planning original garments—original in that I use a collar from one design, and skirt, belt, waist, or sleeve from another, and put these parts of different designs together, making a beautiful harmonious garment.

Earned Every Cent of Tuition

Every once in a while, for the inspiration and encouragement of the woman who wonders if she will be able to meet her payments, we like to publish a letter from some woman who faced the same problem and who solved it by sewing for others. We have hundreds of members who have done this very thing and who are just as pleased and enthusiastic as Mrs. J. H. Peters, one of our Illinois members.

I have found my lessons a great help to me. Although I have always sewed plain things for myself and sisters, I never felt I could undertake to sew for other people; but since taking my Course, different ones have asked me to make things for them. I have made two graduating uniforms for two nurses who graduated last week, and they were so pleased I had to promise to make their spring uniforms. I have made $77 since I joined the Institute, and I earned every cent of my Course myself.

Silk Shirts for Her Sons

A recommendation for any woman's skill as a seamstress that would be very difficult to excel is found in the following letter from Mrs. E. G. Libbert, one of our Indiana members. If there is one person who above another is critical about "homemade" clothing, it is a young man, and the fact that she could satisfactorily make her sons' wedding shirts speaks volumes for her ability, to say nothing about the system of dressmaking that made her accomplishment possible. Mrs. Libbert says:

Each of my boys came to me and asked the favor of my making the silk wedding shirt—"even when we know you are too busy, mother."

The Institute, I think, would have taken a great deal of credit to itself for the wonderful Course it is giving, could it have seen those shirts, for they were perfect in fit, and I drafted every pattern piece used; one, costing me $9, was a replica of an $18 model in Burkhardt's window, Cincinnati.

Full information regarding Courses in Sewing, Dressmaking, Tailoring, Millinery, and Foods and Cookery as taught by the Woman's Institute will be gladly furnished on request by the

Woman's Institute
of Domestic Arts and Sciences, Inc.
DEPT. 21, SCRANTON, PA.

Fashion Service
—— SUPPLEMENT ——

Each Issue of *Vintage Notions Monthly* includes a *Fashion Service Supplement*. You will read about the fashion styles popular in the early twentieth century and receive a collectible fashion illustration to print and frame.

The students of the Woman's Institute would also receive a publication called *Fashion Service*. Where the *Inspiration* newsletter instructed them on all aspects of the domestic arts, not only sewing but also cooking, housekeeping, decorating, etc., *Fashion Service* was devoted entirely to giving current fashions with a key to their development.

Fashion Service prided itself on providing it's readers with reliable style information and the newest fashion forecasting. The publication wasn't just eye candy. The Institute stressed the importance of studying the fashions to benefit the sewer's understanding of dressmaking. To quote founder Mary Brooks Picken, "Once the principles of design...and of construction... are understood, beautiful garments will result. This publication comes to you as an aid to this desired goal. Read the text of every page and reason out the why of every illustration and description that your comprehension of designing and construction may be enlarged and your appreciation made more acute."

Today, these articles and illustrations give us a historically accurate view of what fashion really meant 100 years ago. Not only can we study these articles for an "of-the-time" style snapshot, but just as their students did, we can also learn to understand the principles of design and increase our sewing skills. In each issue, look for a collectible illustration in the back of the supplement!

Full-Skirt Dress

Is it to be wondered that Fashion is so strongly influenced by thoughts of spring's bright skies, colorful meadows, and singing birds that she is inclined to show a wee bit of partiality to youth at this season of the year? Some of us may feel a bit slighted because we do not receive primary consideration, but why not be content to live in anticipation of the next fall and winter season when light colors and fluffy styles will, as usual, be forced into the background by colors more appropriate for winter wear and styles more dignified in line? Winter is generally quite as partial to added years and generous proportions as spring is to youth and slenderness.

Few of the present-day styles show a great variety of trimming, but they seem to favor an abundance of one or two selections. If tucks are employed at all, they are used in great numbers as tiny pin tucks or as a succession of a sufficient number to form almost a complete skirt, provided they are of the wider variety shown in this model. Here, the tucks are left unpressed, a feature noticeable in the softer fabrics.

If embroidery is employed, not one or two single motifs are favored, but, instead, it is used in all-over effect. If buttons are selected, they are applied without stint in long rows.

A word about cape collars or berthas may be of interest. They naturally were revived with the short capes, which are featured on so many jackets and coats or worn with sports dresses. Sometimes they are made just wide enough to carry out their recognized mission of seemingly broadening the shoulders and thus proving especially becoming to slender persons.

Material and Pattern.—What more appropriate material than crêpe de Chine could be used for a frock having unpressed tucks? Its very soft sheen throws the tucks into subdued relief against the skirt background, thus providing a rather elusive shading that is bound to appeal to youthful, esthetic tastes.

As to color, the names borrowed from flowers have evidently been exhausted, for otherwise how could so lowly a vegetable as the onion receive any consideration from designers? But the name is really quite apropos, for this color resembles the rich tan of the ripe or dry onion skin. A pleasing contrast is provided in the hemstitching of the tucks, which is done in bright-blue silk, and in the chain-stitch embroidery of this same color, which is applied with heavy floss to the bertha portions.

For the average figure, 5¾ yards of crêpe de Chine is required. Two spools of blue silk thread for the hemstitching and twelve skeins of matching silk floss for the embroidery should also be provided. No skirt pattern is required for any of the full-skirt styles, as these are made of straight lengths of material. A plain-waist pattern may be used for the waist portion.

To form the pattern for the bertha, experiment with muslin on the person for whom you are making the dress. Pin a lengthwise thread at the center back of the waist, and smooth the material over the shoulders to the natural shoulder line, letting the collar assume a slight flare. Then pin a lengthwise thread of another piece of muslin at the center front, and form the front cape effect in practically the same manner. Cut the neck and outer edges just as you desire to have them, and pin the shoulder seams to make the collar fit properly at this point.

Cutting.—For the skirt, cut two full widths of material, making each of them the desired skirt length, plus allowance for the tucks and hem. In order to estimate the amount of material required for the tucks, first decide on the width you wish to make them; for each tuck allow twice this width and multiply the result by the number of tucks you desire. For instance, if you wish to make seven tucks 2¼ inches wide, determine the allowance required for them by multiplying twice the tuck width, or 4½ inches, by 7, which makes 31½ inches.

Be very careful to cut the skirt widths on an exact crosswise grain of the material, for a skirt of this kind must have the tucks folded on crosswise threads in order to appear well. As a general rule, a skirt that is unshaped at the upper edge is suitable for the type of person to whom the full-skirt dress is becoming. But if there is an appreciable difference in the front and back skirt lengths of the individual, the waist line of the skirt should be curved correspondingly in order to prevent the skirt from cupping at the center front just below the waist line.

Place the center back of the waist pattern about 2 inches from the double selvages, in order to make provision for the overlapping hems required at the center back. Place the bertha pattern with its center front and back on a lengthwise fold.

Construction.—Join the sleeve and waist seams as well as the left shoulder seam of the bertha as French fells. Also, join the two lengths provided for the skirt by means of narrow French seams. Then proceed to baste the skirt tucks in position. First, turn a hem in the lower edge, making this the width that you desire the tucks to be. Then, measuring from the hem, indicate by means of pins or chalk marks the lines on which to turn the tucks, placing these marks far enough apart to allow the space you desire between the tucks. For instance, if you desire 1-inch spaces between 2-inch tucks, place the marks to indicate the lines for turning 7 inches apart, the rule to follow for this work being three times the tuck width, plus the width of the space desired.

If you intend to have the tucks hemstitched, you will find it advantageous to draw threads to indicate the lines on which the tucks are to be secured, for the marking of tuck lines on material as soft as crêpe de Chine is a rather tedious process.

In addition to basting the tucks securely in position, indicate, by means of basting, all the lines you wish to have hemstitched in the sleeves and bertha and have all the hemstitching done. Then to prepare the dress for fitting, make a narrow, continuous placket at the center back of the skirt and gather the upper edge. Also turn and baste the allowance made for hems at the center back of the waist and run a gathering thread in the lower edge. Then make ready a soft inside stay belt.

Fitting.—Hook the stay belt on the figure, closing this belt at the center back. Then put on the waist, adjust the fulness at the waist line, and pin this to the stay belt.

Next, pin the skirt securely to the belting, arranging the side seams so that they appear as a continuation of the under-arm seams of the waist. Observe the line at the lower edge of the skirt; if it appears uneven, either drop or lift the waist line at points where the irregularity occurs.

Give attention next to the insertion and the length of the sleeves. Then place the bertha in position and chalk the line on which the upper portion of the waist is to be cut to make it even with the neck line of the bertha.

Finishing.—Baste and stitch the waist and skirt to the stay belt, clip the raw edges quite close, and cover them with a narrow bias binding, stitching it on both edges. Finish the armhole seams as French fells. Then give attention to the neckline finish. Stitch the neck edges of the bertha and waist together from the left shoulder across the front to the center back; turn these edges back under and cover them with a bias facing. Finish the neck edge of the waist and bertha separately from the left shoulder to the center back, using a bias facing for these edges and also for the shoulder edges of the bertha.

Complete the dress by applying the snap fasteners and making a sash of double lengthwise strips of material that, when sewed together, make a strip about 2½ yards long.

Model 18

Variations of Full-Skirt Dress

Model 18A.—If months have any reasoning powers or feelings at all, what an object of envy June must be among the others! Her complete existence is made up of a succession of happy events, chiefly commencement exercises and weddings, and, naturally, on such occasions much of the style interest for summer centers. Graduates and brides can hardly be put in the same class when clothes requirements are considered. But the linking of class-night and bridesmaid's dresses is quite another matter, for generally a design suitable for the one purpose is truly as appropriate for the other, a statement made quite convincing by this variation of the full-skirt dress.

Changeable taffeta, endive green shading into golden bronze, forms the handkerchief tunics, the broad front girdle section, the back waist panel, and the camisole foundation of the dress, and 13- or 14-inch imitation metallic lace, or metal-thread lace, as it is called, the side skirt and waist portions. There will be needed 3 yards of the taffeta and 6 yards of the lace. In addition, 1 yard of net must be provided for the skirt foundation.

Form the distended-hip effect by draping the lace on the net underskirt, which is four times the width of the lace. Start at the back with one end of the lace even with the lower edge of the skirt and the scalloped edge even wtih the side seam. Let the straight edge of the lace extend without fulness up to the waist line just under the edge of the handkerchief tunic, then with fulness across the side waist line, and again without fulness down the front to the lower edge of the skirt.

For each of the handkerchief tunics, cut a square of full-width material. Apply these so that one corner extends just a trifle below the skirt hem at the center front and center back, in order to cover the joining of the lace, and let the opposite corner extend as far above the waist line as necessary. Adjust the fulness and turn back the corners at each side so that they give the effect that is illustrated. From the triangular portion that extends above the waist line, cut the pointed girdle section.

Model 18B.—Since the mere mention of honeydew melons acts as a stimulant to one's gustatory sense, imagine what would result from a glimpse of this dress of sheer linen, honeydew in color. Charming and youthful are its trimmings of pin tucks, white organdie loops, and rows of ladder work formed by narrow bands of organdie. Decided contrast is afforded by the sash of black ciré ribbon. For the average figure, 3½ yards of linen, 1 yard of organdie, and 2¼ yards of ribbon are required.

To make the loop trimming, double a narrow bias strip and stitch and turn it as you would in making cording; then cut the strip into pieces about 3 inches long. Loop each one of these pieces and baste them close together along the edge, with the ends extending ⅛ inch or more under the edge. Then, at the lower edge of the skirt, apply a facing to cover these ends, extending this to the skirt trimming band. Use double lengthwise strips for the cross-pieces of the ladder work, and secure the ends of these under the bound edges.

Model 18C.—The revival of lace has proved to be more than a passing fancy, for its vogue is still very decided. With white net, shadow lace chose a foundation of pale-pink chiffon for this model; then, to make it typically an afternoon garden frock, it added a number of sash ends of soft-blue ribbon and roses of just the shades that the garden boasts.

Material requirements include 1 yard of net, 2 yards of chiffon, 11 yards of 6-inch lace, and 6½ yards of ribbon.

Form the three panels by cutting straight strips of net about 6 or 7 inches wide and of a length that will permit the lace to extend just below the skirt hem; then round the lower corners of the panels. In applying the lace, supply a sufficient amount of fulness around the curved portion of the panels to prevent the outer edge of the lace from appearing drawn.

Model 18D.—A new conceit in dotted Swiss is the introduction of such deep colors as brown, navy, red, violet, and even black. Although used for many frocks, these colors are not quite so summery as the average dress likes to appear on warm days. Therefore, we can appreciate the reason for the selection of the more conservative shade of rose for this model. The center-shirred, picoted ruffles and the collar are of white organdie, the lace that trims the vestee is of the filet variety, and the sash is of rose-and-black, double-faced ribbon.

As dotted Swiss is only 30 inches wide, two and one-half widths must be provided for this full-skirt model and allowance made for a hem to extend to the first row of ruffles. In all, 5 yards of dotted Swiss, 1¼ yards of organdie, ¼ yard of lace, and 2¼ yards of ribbon are required for the average person.

Form the collar pattern by experimenting with muslin. Pin the muslin with a lengthwise thread at the center-back neck line. Then draw the material around toward the front, making it assume the high roll effect that is illustrated, and to emphasize this effect further, pin a small dart at the back neck line. Cut the outer edge and the neck lines to shape them as you desire.

Model 18E.—Suggestive of a past generation, when sheer cotton trimmed with Val lace and insertion was all that even the most extravagant young maiden displayed on so momentous an occasion as her graduation, is this exquisitely dainty and youthful dress of white batiste.

In previous years, fine fabric and yards of insertion, with little thought given to the amount of labor involved in putting them together, constituted the extravagance. Today, the cost of fabric and trimming is of minor importance compared with the hand and detail work, which, if skilfully applied, adds to the intrinsic value of the dress. All of which goes to prove that the modern girl who would be distinctively dressed for her graduation exercises should consider herself very fortunate if she may appear in a model such as this—an up-to-date replica of her grandmother's charm and simplicity.

For this model, 3½ yards of batiste, 16 yards of Val insertion, 14½ yards of lace, and 2¼ yards of ribbon are required.

A long-waisted blouse pattern may be used for cutting this design. In order to form the pointed effect at the back, make an extension below the waist line of the pattern. Then, from the width of material provided for the back portion of the skirt, cut out a V section at the waist line, making this of the depth of the V formed in the waist.

With chalk or basting, mark lines to indicate the correct position for the rows of insertion. Begin at the lower edge to apply the rows of insertion so that the upper curved row may be lapped over the others. Attach the sash at the under-arm seams of the bodice where the insertion starts to slant.

Model 18F.—A group of youthful dresses is indeed incomplete this season unless it includes an Eton suggestion and a touch of smocking, features that are so effectively combined in this design. The material is caramel-colored crêpe de Chine, the sash of tortoise-brown velvet ribbon appliquéd at the front with crêpe-de-Chine roses, the smocking of brown, and the vestee and cuffs of Swiss embroidery edging.

Under-arm extensions of the back of the blouse are evident. These are held in position by self-covered buttons. Bands of pin tucks in the skirt are separated by a 2-inch tuck. The hem is made deep enough to reach the lowest pin tuck.

For this model, provide 4¼ yards of crêpe de Chine, 3 yards of velvet ribbon, ⅞ yard of Swiss embroidery, and ½ yard of net or 1 yard of light-weight silk for the waist lining.

As the Eton effect does not extend to the waist line, the lower edge of the waist lining should be faced with a 3- or 4-inch band of the dress material.

18 A

18 B

18 C

18 D

18 E

18 F

Circular-Skirt Dress

Rumors of an approaching vogue for circular skirts have extended over so long a period without any important evidence of their materializing that there seemed danger of these rumors degenerating into the "Wolf! Wolf!" class. But while it is certain that the flaring skirt will not be the most widely accepted type this spring, that it will be of undeniable interest among many other types is not doubted.

This model is significant, not only because of its circular skirt but also because of its tendency toward princesse lines. The princesse type is very promising and will undoubtedly receive a goodly share of attention for some time to come, as nipped-in waists cannot remain much longer in the background. It must not be concluded, however, that a closely fitted effect at the waist line is necessary in the princesse styles, for the designs that have been introduced thus far do not follow the lines of the figure closely. Rather, they curve in just enough to suggest the fitted effect, which is further emphasized if the flare skirt is used in connection with it.

According to present style standards, the difference between a distinctive and an ordinary-appearing frock of this type often lies in the fitting. If the dress is made too snug at the waist line or over the hips, it does not have the appearance of ease and grace that is so essential. This same suggestion may be applied to a dress in which the circular skirt is cut separate from the blouse. In this case, the skirt should be attached to a lining or a blouse that is as straight in line as a chemise frock.

Material and Pattern.—Twilled materials seem to be the most favored of the medium-weight woolen fabrics, and, from the standpoint of service and smartness, almost any of the varieties may be chosen without hesitancy. Poiret twill in pelican gray is the material of which this model was developed. The embroidery is carried out in gray silk floss of a slightly lighter tone, with the addition of gold metallic thread. The arrangement of the embroidery on the front and back suggests a long-waisted bodice and for most types makes the dress more becoming than a severely simple princesse model. Embroidery in similar design is repeated for a sleeve trimming. The collar and vestee are of white satin.

Only 3 yards of 54-inch material is required for cutting a style such as this for the average figure. In addition, 1 yard of matching silk or very light-weight satine should be provided for the skirt facing, and ¾ yard of satin for the collar and vestee.

A circular princesse pattern is necessary for the foundation; on this may be marked the oval neck line and the side-front and back sections, which extend from the shoulder on practically a straight line to several inches below the waist line and then on a gradual curve to the side seam line.

Cutting.—Fold the material lengthwise through the center, and place the long front and back pattern portions on the material so that the center front and back are on the fold and the lower skirt edge of one is a seam's width from one cut end and the corresponding edge of the other pattern portion is a seam's width from the opposite cut end, thus bringing the neck edge of each pattern portion near the center of the material. Then place the sleeve and side waist sections on that portion of the material which extends along the selvage between the flaring lines of the front and back patterns.

Before removing the pattern pieces, mark all the seam lines very carefully, for accurate seam lines are of the utmost importance in a tailored garment. For the small sash ends, cut four strips on a bias that follows the twill of the fabric, making each about 22 inches long and 2½ or 3 inches wide.

For the collar, cut a bias strip of satin about 1 yard long and 8 inches wide at each end, sloping to 6 inches at the center.

Construction and Fitting.—First join the under-arm sections to the front and back dress portions, using small basting-stitches for this purpose and leaving the upper end of the left front seam open. Then turn the seam edges of the front toward the center front and those of the back toward the center back, clipping the upper seam edge at intervals through the curved portion so that it will lie perfectly flat, and baste the shoulder and under-arm seams. Also, baste the sleeve seams.

Then try on the dress and give very special attention to the fitting. If the skirt fulness seems to fall toward the front, try lifting the dress just a trifle at the sides. Do not fit the dress very closely over the bust, be even more lenient in fitting the hips, and permit only a suggestion of an inward curve at the waist line. See that the armhole curve is rather high at the shoulder and that the sleeve fits with moderate ease. Provided you find it necessary to make any changes, mark the new seam lines very accurately, curving and shaping them properly.

At this time, fold through the center lengthwise the strip of material that has been provided for the collar. Pin the center of this to the center front of the neck or vest line, placing the fold at the outside. Then proceed to pin the collar to the remainder of the neck line. Along the lower curved portion, hold the inner edge of the strip as full as possible without making it appear gathered and stretch the corresponding outer edge to make the collar lie more nearly flat. Apply the remainder of the strip in an easy manner, and cut away the surplus material at the center back not required for seams and an overlap. With the collar fitted in this manner, pin over the raw edges a strip that may afterward be used for a binding, so that the collar may be made separate from the dress and merely tacked in position, thus facilitating its removal for cleaning.

Mark the length required for the opening at the left side front and the points at which to secure the sash ends; then remove the dress from the figure.

Finishing.—Before stitching the side seams, make the sash ends, insert them at the points indicated by the pins, and baste them in position. Next, join the under-arm sections to the front and back dress portions by means of plain seams. Then press the seam edges toward the center, as they were turned in the fitting. Use plain, pressed-open seams for the shoulder and under-arm edges and plain seams with the edges pressed back on the waist for the armholes. Finish the raw edges by means of overcasting or binding.

Next, apply embroidery of the design illustrated or according to some other design. Then face the left shoulder and side-front waist opening, the neck line, and also the lower edge of the sleeves by means of bias strips of light-weight silk. Use extreme care in applying these facings, so that their use will not be evident from the right side.

With the dress in this condition, place it on a coat hanger and give it an opportunity to sag for a day or more. You will find it advantageous to follow this suggestion before hanging any circular skirt, for almost all materials are apt to sag in a moderate or marked degree through the decidedly bias portions.

After hanging the skirt, trim the lower edge to within a generous seam's width of the line marked for the hem turn; then cut a fitted facing of light-weight silk for the lower edge of the skirt, shaping it exactly the same as the skirt edge and making it about 4 inches wide. Apply this with care, in order to make it as inconspicuous as possible.

Finish the collar and vestee and tack these in position. Apply snap fasteners to the center-back closing of the collar, along the neck line of the collar and dress from the center back to the left shoulder seam, and then along the shoulder seam and the side-front closing of the dress.

Model 19

Variations of Circular-Skirt Dress

Model 19A.—Besides the novelty of the slightly circular skirt, this blue-serge model offers other unusual features in the soft green cloth used for the vestee and skirt trimming band, the matching green fringe applied to the lower edge of the skirt, and the black satin tie knotted at the front in modified middy-tie fashion. The collar and cuffs are of white satin; the embroidery is of black braid and floss.

Requirements for the average figure are 3 yards of 50- or 54-inch material, ¾ yard or 50- or 54-inch cloth for trimming, ⅜ yard of satin for the collar and cuffs, 2½ yards of fringe, 10 yards of ½-inch braid, and 2 skeins of silk floss.

A two-piece circular-skirt pattern having side-seam lines, a comparatively loose basque-waist pattern, and either a plain one-piece sleeve pattern or one having a dart from the wrist to the elbow are the ones that are required. By experimenting, determine how deep you wish to make the pointed effect at the back; then extend the back portion of the waist pattern to produce this effect and on the back portion of the circular-skirt pattern outline a point of the same dimensions, exercising the greatest care in this work so as to insure a correctly fitting garment.

Allow about 1 inch for the finish at the lower edge of the skirt. Do not cut the trimming band until you have sewed the skirt seams and have hung the skirt up for a day or so to permit it to sag. Then mark the correct line for turning the lower edge; that is, "hang" the skirt and cut away the lower edge to within ½ or ¾ inch of the marked line. Form a pattern for the trimming band by outlining the lower edge of the skirt on a piece of paper of sufficient size. Cut the band in two parts, arranging for seams that will be over those in the skirt and making the band the width you desire.

After joining the band with plain pressed-open seams, apply it by placing its right side to the wrong side of the skirt, lower edges even, stitching on the marked line of the skirt, and then turning the band to the right side, letting it extend just a trifle, about ⅟₁₆ inch, below the joining line. Finish the upper edge by stitching one row of braid flat over the raw edge or by turning the raw edge under and slip-stitching it. Form the zigzag braided border, as illustrated; then, with silk floss, supply the embroidery lines that extend up from the braid, using some sort of knot-stitch or a twisted running-stitch for this work.

Model 19B.—Black taffeta's affinity for organdie is evidenced by any number of lovely spring models that show either a combination of these materials or the organdie used more sparingly, merely as a trimming.

In this design, the organdie is used for one of the prettiest collars the season offers, a rolled-cape style trimmed with puffings of self-material edged with Val insertion and the outer row of insertion finished with a picoted ruffle of self-material. A puffing formed in a similar manner provides the sleeve finish and another bit of organdie appears in the gathered vestee. Odd-figured ribbon emphasizes the scalloped outline of the circular tunics, and very simple embroidered-rose motifs developed in black-silk floss add further decoration.

Provided the upper part of the underskirt of this design is made of a lining fabric, 5 yards of taffeta will prove sufficient. For the lining, 1½ yards of China silk or other lining material is required. For the trimming illustrated, 6½ yards of ¾-inch ribbon, 1 yard of organdie, 3½ yards of insertion, 2¼ yards of lace, and 8 skeins of silk floss must be supplied.

To develop the circular tunic patterns, first outline the tunics on a plain-skirt pattern of the kind suitable for cutting the underskirt. Trace these tunic sections and then, to provide the flare, slash each section lengthwise in a number of places and separate the pieces at the lower edge an amount sufficient to give the flare you desire. Separate the pieces just a trifle at the waist line, provided you wish a little fulness at this point.

Cut the lower portion of the underskirt long enough to extend several inches under the lower tunic section, and the remainder of the underskirt of lining material. Attach the skirt to the waist lining; also, join the sleeves to this lining and arrange the waist closing at the right shoulder and under arm.

Model 19C.—A patchwork-quilt motif furnished inspiration for the trimming of this dress of pearl-gray taffeta and thus added a touch that has a decided appeal. But the gray taffeta and colored patchwork motifs are not the only attractive features of this design. The rolled organdie collar with its odd side closing and the single sash end, which starts at the left under-arm seam and is continued across the back and looped and knotted at the right under-arm seam, provide details that are sure to please.

Coral is the predominating color in the patchwork motifs, which are made of wool. Soft blue and green are also prominent, and other harmonizing colors are noted in the silk floss used for blanket-stitching the motifs in position. Bits of taffeta or organdie might be used in place of the wool, and a single bright color or a combination of colors employed.

The frock is one that is particularly suitable for rather youthful and slender types and would be just as attractive if made entirely of organdie. For the average figure, provide 4¼ yards of the dress fabric and ¾ yard of organdie for collar and cuffs, both estimates including a sufficient amount for bindings.

Cut the waist with the aid of a semifitting long-waisted pattern, and the skirt with a slightly flaring circular pattern that has some fulness at the waist line. Cut the sash about 60 inches long and from 6 to 8 inches wide.

Form the collar pattern by experimenting with muslin, arranging it to produce the effect you wish. You will find that the collar appears best if made of a 7- or 8-inch bias strip, which is fitted into the neck line and shaped at the side front.

Model 19D.—Combining a rather severe or tailored effect with elaborate embroidery and making the result pleasing is no small task, but all this, yes more, has been accomplished in this charming model of serge embroidered in metallic gold. The bodice is in long-waisted and rather close-fitting basque effect. The pointed line of the bodice is repeated in the skirt embroidery, and the flare in the cuff is merely a repetition of the circular effect in the skirt. An applied band cut in one with the cuff extends through the center of the sleeve and across the shoulder line and terminates at the neck.

Both very slender and stout persons must be content to let the average type have monopoly of this style, for the severity of the bodice lines would prove trying for nearly all slender figures, while the arrangement of the embroidery and the emphasis given to the width of the front bust line make the design inadvisable for a stout person.

For the average figure, provide 3½ yards of serge 54 inches wide, or 4 yards 40 inches wide, and 20 skeins of floss. Silk floss of blue, henna, tomato, gray, or black may be substituted for the metallic thread. Also, the dress may be made of tricotine or soft cloth in blue, tan, or gray and harmonizing silk floss embroidery applied.

In order to cut the sleeve trimming band, pin to the center of the cuff a strip of paper about 1¾ inches wide and long enough to extend from the cuff to the neck line. Place the pattern on the materials so that the lengthwise center of the cuff, and likewise of the strip, is on a true bias grain. Provide a seam allowance on all edges. In applying the strip, fit it carefully over the shoulders. Arrange the opening by finishing the left-front shoulder, armhole, and under-arm lines free from the lining, and the left-sleeve trimming band so that it may be secured after the shoulder seam is fastened.

19A

19B

19C

Sports Dress

Last year it seemed as if sports clothes had reached the very zenith of their possibilities as well as popularity. The latitude in the kinds of materials recognized as suitable for sports wear and the leniency in regard to the purpose and use of sports costumes were taken as sufficient reasons for presuming that another summer season could hardly outrival the preceding one. Was it the conclusiveness of our presumptions that put Fashion "on her mettle" and made her determined to produce the extraordinary? At any rate, she has accomplished this in her delightful sports offerings for spring and summer, and the very least we astonished onlookers can do is to make the most of the opportunities she is presenting.

Of the materials that are being used for sports costumes, the new weaves of silk are the most fascinating. The majority of these are crêpe-like in character, medium heavy in weight, novel in design, and of a shimmering quality that is not evident in many of the other silks sanctioned for spring wear. Tricolette in new and delightful weaves is used for many sports skirts and capes. In addition, Canton crêpe and crêpe de Chine, because of their versatile character, are borrowed from the list suggested for other purposes.

Of the woolens, there are jersey and homespun weaves and coatings of rough character, in addition to white serge and white and bright-colored flannels, these last two materials being used in abundance.

Of the cottons, there are the heavy novelty weaves, many of them twilled, considerable ratine or homespun, and hop sacking.

Of the linens, the heavier weaves are, of course, the most desirable for sports wear. A pronounced vogue for linen is promised, and in anticipation of this many cotton-and-linen mixtures have been produced to sell at prices within reach of the average purse. These mixtures have a particular virtue in their close resemblance to all-linen and their lessened tendency to crush readily.

Sports costumes of various descriptions are included in the showing for spring and summer, but as the sports dress with loose overblouse and comfortably wide skirt is the type that is most practical for the majority of girls and women, this model receives detailed consideration.

Although the straight silhouette seems to be of primary importance in sports apparel, skirts are by no means scant, for fulness is almost invariably provided by plaits, sometimes merely a few inconspicuous ones of the inverted style, but more often accordion or knife plaits, as in this model, which take up all the skirt material. Circular skirts, too, are in evidence.

The blouse lines of this model are suitable for the majority of persons, provided the plaited peplum portion is made the length most becoming to the individual type. If made for more than average proportions, the style would perhaps prove more becoming with the waist-line embroidery omitted.

Material and Pattern.—A heavy quality of rose-colored satin-faced crêpe was chosen for the blouse of this model. The skirt of white Canton crêpe has little to prove its relationship to the blouse, unless the very narrow band of rose-colored crêpe placed at the lower edge is convincing evidence. The embroidery on the flare cuffs and the sash of the blouse is of white wool. The buttons on the blouse are covered with the rose-colored crêpe, and those on the skirt, with white. Material requirements for the average figure include 2¾ yards of rose-colored crêpe, 3½ yards of white crêpe, 5 skeins of white yarn, and ½ yard of China silk for a camisole lining.

The only patterns required for this dress are a plain waist and sleeve, a collar that turns back with the waist fronts, and a flare cuff. The peplum portion of the blouse and the skirt are made of straight sections of material.

Cutting.—If you wish to have the skirt knife-plaited, provide two widths of material, each of a skirt length, plus an inch or so for seam allowance. For the plaited peplum, cut two widths of the satin-faced crêpe, making each of the length you desire the peplum portion, plus an allowance of 1 inch for a hem. Also, cut two crosswise strips for the trimming band at the lower edge of the skirt, making these about 2 inches wide, so that, when applied, they will be more than 1 inch wide.

In cutting the waist, place the center front of the pattern 3 inches from the selvage, so as to allow for the facing, which is evident when the upper fronts are turned back. For the belt, cut a straight strip 8 or 10 inches longer than the waist measurement and about 6 inches wide. Also, cut a camisole waist lining.

Construction.—First of all, prepare the skirt for steam plaiting by joining all but one of the lengthwise seams. Make these as plain pressed-open seams, and clip the edges at several points to prevent them from drawing when the material is plaited. Also, apply the contrasting band to the lower edge of the skirt, first placing it with its right side to the wrong side of the skirt and stitching a seam's width from the edge, and then pressing the band back on the right side, turning under the upper edge of the band and either stitching or slip-stitching this in place.

After the skirt is plaited, stitch the remaining seam, taking care to match the plaits exactly, so that the seam will not be conspicuous. Also, make the camisole lining.

Next, give attention to the blouse. Join the seams in the usual manner and turn back the front facings and baste them in position. Turn a hem along the lower edge of the peplum portion. Then lay in the plaits, making them rather shallow, so that they will not produce too much bulk at the hip line, and forming a box plait at the center front.

Fitting.—Put the camisole lining on the figure and shape it a trifle by pinning a very small dart from the waist line to the bust at each side of the front. As the camisole and skirt are to be made together in slip-over style, the waist line must be made loose enough to permit this foundation to be slipped on and off with ease. Pin the skirt to the camisole, "hanging" it from the waist line so as to make it perfectly even at the bottom.

Next, put on the blouse and observe the points generally noted in the fitting. Then pin the peplum portion in position, taking care not to secure the pins through the skirt and camisole underneath. Arrange for the peplum opening on the under edge of the front box plait, slashing the material at this point.

Finishing.—Finish the waist line of the skirt and camisole by basting and stitching on the pinned line and then covering the raw edge of the skirt with a bias facing. Also, stitch the peplum to the blouse, bringing the seam edges to the right side.

Make the belt and cuffs ready for application by embroidering them. Then fold the embroidered strip for the belt lengthwise through the center, with the right sides together. Stitch together the lengthwise edges; then turn the belt to the right side and finish each end by turning the raw edges to the inside of the belt and slip-stitching the edges together. After the cuffs are embroidered, face them with self-material and apply the cuffs and collar as suggested for the plain blouse, which is considered in the dressmaking lessons.

Tack the belt to the dress, arranging the opening at the under-arm seam, and cover the raw edges underneath the belt at the side-front waist line with a narrow bias facing. Also, bind the slashed edges of the peplum portion.

Complete the dress by making and applying self-covered loops to the blouse opening, sewing the buttons to the blouse and skirt, and applying the snap fasteners.

Model 20

Sports Costumes

Model 20A.—Naturally, the American longing for color is pronounced. At least, this is the claim of authorities who have studied the color likings of people living in various climates and have concluded that personal or racial fondness for bright colors is in proportion to the warmness of the climate. Thus, in hot climates where Nature's coloring in flowers and vegetation is vivid, the natives show a passionate fondness for bright colors, while in the frozen north, where white and neutral tones prevail in the landscape, the native preference is for subdued colors. Living between these two extremes, we should, according to this rule, have a liking for color that is much stronger than is indicated by the clothes that we generally wear.

Perhaps a national restraining impulse is responsible for this condition, for proof of our love of color is noted in the abandon and enthusiasm with which we select materials for sports wear, sometimes in one brilliant color and at other times in a combination of colors such as those used for this model.

The loosely belted overblouse, or coat, is of cretonne in green, violet, and capucine, or nasturtium, colors that shade into brown, none of these really glaring colors, but of sufficient brightness to make them interesting. The trimming is of brown grosgrain ribbon, while the skirt is of tan crêpe de Chine, light and unobstrusive as to tone, thus emphasizing the loveliness of the colors in the jacket rather than detracting from them. The small box plaits are of the machine-made variety. For the average figure, provide 2½ yards of cretonne, 2¼ yards of crêpe de Chine, and 5 yards of grosgrain ribbon about 1½ inches wide.

A plain overblouse or coat pattern may be used for cutting this model. The construction is very simple. First join the seams in the usual manner; then bind all the edges with ribbon. To form the collar, tack a strip of ribbon at each side of the neck, letting this fall over the belt, as the illustration indicates; then place another strip around the neck line and tack this in place over the strips that were secured at the side.

Model 20B.—Green of the very newest and freshest grass variety is the color chosen for the long overblouse of this crêpe-de-Chine sports costume. The foundation follows the precedent early established that a sports skirt, especially if worn with a bright-colored overblouse, must be of white or a light, neutral tone. Made as a camisole slip with straps over the shoulders, the foundation might hang on practically straight lines and permit ample freedom of motion, a commendable quality in a sports costume. However, an entire slip is not necessary, for the skirt may be made separate and the overblouse supplied with a vest of the skirt material. For this purpose, 2⅛ yards of white crêpe de Chine will be sufficient. The overblouse requires 2½ yards of crêpe de Chine, with about a dozen strings of white beads for the embroidery.

The dart, which is shown just below the side-front waist line of the blouse, is an interesting feature, as it permits some of the front under-arm length to be removed and the line at the lower edge thus made less decidedly curved.

Model 20C.—That young folk need have no monopoly on cross-stitching as a dress trimming is evidenced by this frock of soft-pink ratine, on which navy-blue cross-stitching is used with such good effect. Another touch of blue is provided by the linen used for the collar and the trimming bands of the waist, sleeve, and skirt. The buttons are covered with the linen.

This dress may be made as a two-piece model, foundation waist and sleeve and straight gathered skirt patterns being used in the cutting; or, it may be made as a one-piece model and a simple one-piece dress pattern employed. In either case, about 3½ yards of ratine and ½ yard of linen will be required for the average figure. For the embroidery, 6 skeins of floss will prove sufficient.

Model 20D.—Plaids seem to appear at their very best when combined with plain material, for the solid color affords relief from the geometric division of colors in the plaid design. This same regularity in the plaid makes it advisable to vary its use, as in the application of bias, and not to depend on the straight-cut fabric alone to provide all the diversity that is necessary. A promiscuous use of bias, however, is disconcerting rather than pleasing, so it should be applied cautiously.

In this woolen sports suit, straight plaid is used for the skirt and the scarf collar, and bias for the sleeve facings, the cuff effect at the lower edge of the coat, and the pocket bindings. Henna shades predominate in the coloring of the plaid, and plain-colored henna in a light-weight woolen fabric similar to flannel is used for the jacket. Of 54-inch material, 1½ yards of the plain color and 2⅛ yards of the plaid are required.

In cutting the material, first provide the straight strip for the scarf, taking this from one selvage edge and making it about 10 inches wide and 40 inches long, or longer, if you prefer.

Make the skirt of straight pieces of material, providing the width you desire and matching the plaids carefully on the seam lines. Turn the lower edge on a crosswise thread of the material, so that the plaid will appear even at the bottom, and if any adjustment of the skirt length is required to make the skirt hang properly, shape the waist line to accomplish this.

As the bias band at the lower edge of the blouse does not fit the hips closely, the jacket may be made as a slip-over model and the center-front opening not extended through the band.

Model 20E.—When a material as colorful and glossy as sports satin in a tangerine shade is used for a blouse and this is embroidered rather elaborately, the lines must of necessity be very simple in order not to make the general effect too ornate. As illustrated, the embroidery is of white wool applied in all-over, French-knot effect to the front skirt portion of the blouse and made to extend in a point above the waist line. A similar treatment is applied to the sleeves. Embroidery of this kind requires a great deal of time if applied by hand, but with the use of a small embroidery machine of the kind that is popular at the present time, it can be worked very quickly. The skirt is of white silk crêpe; this, also, is absolutely plain as to line.

An excellent quality of cotton crêpe might be used in place of sports satin, and ratine or imitation linen employed for the skirt. Of any of these materials, 2⅛ yards will be required for the skirt and 2⅛ yards for the blouse, while 25 skeins or 1 ball of wool will be needed for the embroidery.

Model 20F.—Decidedly the newest feature of sports costumes is the shoulder cape, which is so exclusive in nature that, properly, its use is limited to one dress. It is not always made of the same color or even of the same fabric as the dress, but invariably it is harmonious in texture, color, line, and trimming and distinctively a part of the dress it completes.

In this instance, the cape is of flamingo-pink wool with trimming of white flannel. The dress is a long-waisted, slip-over style of white flannel with waist-line embroidery of flamingo-colored yarn and pockets bound with the cape material. For the average figure, 1 yard of 54-inch material is sufficient for making the cape and ¾ yard for the trimming. The dress can be made out of 3 yards of 40-inch material.

Form the cape pattern by experimenting with muslin. Pin a straight thread at the center back, bring the material over the shoulder, and pin a dart at this point to make the cape fit properly. Then shape the neck line and cut the front on a grain that gives the amount of flare you desire. You will probably find that a slightly bias grain at the front will prove satisfactory. In cutting the material, place the center back of the pattern on a lengthwise fold so as to make a seam unnecessary.

20 A

20 D

20 B

20 C

20 E

20 F

Directoire Dress

A hastily dressed type of woman said when the Directoire was heralded this season, "It is not my kind of costume, for one has to be completely chic to wear it becomingly." In a goodly measure this is true, for the departure from Fashion's regular path is evident when a Directoire costume is worn. Thus attention is attracted to the individual, making careful grooming and great pains as to becomingness totally necessary.

But the mere fact that a typical Directoire costume is becoming to only this one type, which seemingly expresses comparative youthfulness, is no indication that there is nothing of interest or value in Directoire influence for all the other types. Quite the reverse of this is true, for there are details of the Directoire that may be adapted easily and with excellent effect to the extreme types, that is, to stout and slender figures. The broad collars and revers copied from the coats worn by the men of the Directoire period and the Empire waist line, a point noticeable in the women's gowns, are commendable features for the average slender person, while the long lines and semifitted effects may be copied almost exactly by the stout woman.

Just how long the Directoire influence will be felt is a point difficult to forecast, but this fact is apparent: it is a marked diversity from the sort of style we have grown accustomed to, and, as an answer to the oft-repeated request for something new, it has already been enthusiastically accepted.

Many of the spring costumes, even those conceived before the Directoire influence was felt, are developed in such a manner that they have the appearance of suits when, in reality, they are dresses; and in some cases just the reverse of this is true, for what appears to be a dress for street or informal wear, is found, upon investigation, to be a suit with lined jacket.

This Directoire model, which is considered as the feature dress, has a very close resemblance to a suit and might be made, if preferred, with the jacket portion separate. In this case, the development should follow the general rules for the construction of tailored suits, workmanship a little more complicated in detail and the addition of a lining being required.

Material and Pattern.—Navy serge, that ever-reliable and universally favored fabric, is used for this model. The jabot and the wrist-line frills, features as distinctly Directoire as the cut of the garment, are of white batiste. The upper end of the jabot is finished with a bow of black ciré ribbon. For the average figure, provide 4 yards of serge 50 or 54 inches wide, 3/8 yard of batiste, and 2/3 yard of 2-inch ribbon.

An overdress, or jacket, pattern having the broad revers in one with the front and the back in three pieces, with seams extending from the center of the back armhole to the lower edge, a large roll collar, a close-fitting sleeve, and a straight two-piece skirt pattern are required for the cutting of this model.

In order to develop a pattern for the jacket portion with the plain waist as a foundation, slash the front portion of the pattern lengthwise from the center of the shoulder line, separate the pieces from a point just above the bust line to the shoulder in order to form a dart, and overlap them at the lower edge to take out as much fulness at the waist line as seems necessary. Then mark the surplice line and the seam lines on the back portion of the pattern and cut a muslin model, leaving ample material beyond the surplice lines to form the revers and cutting the muslin to extend 18 to 22 inches below the waist line. When fitting the muslin model, shape the back seams to make the jacket fit as closely as you desire, turn back the allowance made for the revers, and mark and cut them of the shape and size you prefer; then cut away the fronts from a slightly raised waist line to the lower edge of the jacket, first marking them to insure accuracy. Form the roll collar pattern, also, by experimenting with muslin.

Cutting.—Place the center back of the jacket and collar patterns on a lengthwise fold of the fabric, and the center of the side-back section and the center-front line of the front section over a lengthwise thread of the fabric. Place the sleeve and skirt patterns on the material in the usual manner. Then cut out all the dress sections, making a generous allowance for seams. Cut facings for the revers on exactly the same grain of the material as the revers, and make these facings wide enough to extend on the under side from 1/2 to 1 inch beyond the line on which the revers are folded.

Construction.—Join the skirt sections by means of plain pressed-open seams, leaving the upper end of the left seam open and finishing this with a bound or flat-stitched continuous placket. Then gather the upper edge of the skirt. Baste the side-back and center-back sections of the jacket together; then baste the shoulder and under-arm seams. Also, baste the sleeve seams, including the dart, if one has been provided in the sleeves.

Fitting.—Adjust the waist-line fulness of the lining to the inside stay belt, arranging the opening of both of these at the center front. Then secure the skirt to the belting and turn up the lower edge of the skirt, making it of the length you desire.

In fitting the jacket portion, observe, in addition to the usual details, the curve of the side-back seams, the lines of the open portion at the center front, and the shape of the revers. Also, pin the collar in position to make sure that it is of the correct shape and size. Last of all, turn up the lower edge of the jacket so as to make an even line at the bottom. This line should be exactly parallel with the skirt hem.

Finishing.—Use plain pressed-open seams throughout the dress and finish them with overcasting or silk-seam binding. Apply the front facings by placing them with their right sides toward the right side of the jacket and the outer edges even and then basting them carefully in position. If the material does not seem to have sufficient body to hold the revers in place properly, an interlining should be used. Cut this of lawn or very light-weight cambric that has been shrunk, make it the same shape as the facings, and baste this over the facing. Stitch around the outside edges, securing the interlining and the facing at the same time.

Then clip the seam allowance at the corner, trim the interlining seam edge to within 1/8 inch of the stitching and the other seam edges to make the facing a trifle narrower than the revers itself, so that the bulk of these edges will be distributed and not cause a pronounced ridge on the right side. Next, turn the facing back over the wrong side of the material, shape the corners properly, and baste around the outside edge, keeping the seam line directly on the edge. Then press the revers and finish the inside edge of the facing by merely catch-stitching the raw edges in position or covering them with a narrow silk facing.

Follow practically this same method in making and applying the collar.

In finishing the hems of the jacket portion, as well as the one in the skirt, instead of making the second turn in the usual manner, stitch one edge of silk seam binding over the raw edge of the hem, but not through to the right side. Then secure the other edge of the seam binding, which extends a trifle beyond the raw edge of the hem, by whipping it to the garment. Finish the waist-line edge of the opening with a silk facing. Arrange the closing of the jacket portion by making a bound buttonhole and attaching large self-covered buttons.

Tack the jacket portion to the lining at the neck and shoulder seams so as to hold it in the correct position on the figure. Also, tack the vestee and frills in position.

Model 21

Variations of Directoire Dress

Model 21A.—To combine an abundance of decidedly new features in one dress and at the same time produce an effect neither startling nor lacking in good taste is really a master achievement—just the sort of achievement that this model displays. The dress is cut without a seam at the front waist line and tapers in just a trifle at the under arm, thus giving a mere suggestion of the princesse. The skirt lines of the overdress are flared to a moderate extent, and additional fulness is provided by the box plaits, which extend from the neck line to the lower edge of the overdress at the center back.

Blue piquetine, a woolen fabric that is similar in appearance to tricotine, but of a finer, lovelier weave, is the material of which the overdress is made, while black satin is used for the underskirt. The collar is of cream-colored satin, but it might be made of the skirt material if desired. Bound buttonholes trim one side of the overdress, and self-covered buttons, the opposite side, while the lower edge is finished with a narrow braided border of very simple design.

This model might be made even more suggestive of the Directoire period if the waist line were raised several inches. Do not cut the dress with a raised waist line, however, until you have determined whether this is becoming to the person for whom the dress is intended and have decided what height of waist line is most pleasing. The substitution of an underskirt of green Canton crêpe in place of black satin would make the appearance of the dress very striking.

To make the style suitable in every respect for the stout woman, omit the extreme collar and use a narrow shawl style of black satin or of self-material.

A style of this kind developed, as illustrated, for the average figure requires 2½ yards of material 50 or 54 inches wide, 2⅛ yards of satin for the underskirt, ½ yard of satin for the collar, and 15 yards of braid.

For cutting the dress, use a one-piece, semifitted pattern, outline on this the cut-away effect at the center front, the front under-arm section, and the box plait at the center back. Cut the strip for the box plaits separate from the skirt, and insert it between the side-back skirt portions.

Model 21B.—In comparison with some of the elaborately embroidered models that are shown in such abundance this spring, this wren-colored tricotine dress, which has borrowed Directoire simplicity, gives one a feeling of decided relief.

The dress is in one piece and has a broad surplice closing, thus giving the wrap-skirt effect that is noted in many separate skirts. The revers are of practically the same shape as those of the feature dress, and may be developed in much the same manner. In place of the high-rolled collar of self-material, however, this model has a delightfully becoming collar formed of three rows of ecru-organdie frilling built on a straight foundation of this same material. Also, of marked interest is the rosette of brown satin used to finish the ends of the narrow satin belt. This rosette is formed of double, petal-shaped pieces secured at the center to a covered mold or cabochon.

For the average figure, provide 2¾ yards of tricotine 50 or 54 inches wide, 1¼ yards of organdie frilling or ½ yard of organdie, and ½ yard of satin.

A simple one-piece dress pattern having a surplice extension may be used for the cutting of this model. Give very close attention to the finishing of the dress, for the simplicity of the trimming will make noticeable any defect in the workmanship.

If the material used for the dress is not of very heavy weight, the flare cuffs may be made double; otherwise, they should be lined with light-weight silk of self-color. Use matching silk, also, for facing the lapped curved edge of the skirt, or bind this edge with bias self-material and extend the binding around the lower edge of the skirt.

Model 21C.—Quaker demureness and Directoire smartness both have such a decided appeal in this model that it is difficult to determine which feature is more fascinating. The fabric is duvetyn in a deep shade of gray, the knife-plaited front skirt portion of crêpe de Chine in a matching shade of gray, and the collar and flared turn-back cuffs of white satin. This model would be attractive also if made of dark-blue cloth with an inserted front portion of black satin.

A dress of this style requires, for the average figure, 3¾ yards of fabric 40 inches wide, with 1½ yards of crêpe for the plaited-skirt portion and 1 yard of satin for the double collar and cuffs.

In making the dress, turn a 5-inch hem at one end of the piece provided for the front skirt portion and vestee, and have this length plaited. Then secure the plaited section to the upper part of the waist lining in order that it may form the vestee effect illustrated. Tack the plaited portions to each side front of the dress, leaving the left side open to a point several inches below the waist line, so as to provide an opening for the dress. The opening of the waist lining, also, should be arranged at this point.

Finish the opening at the center front of the dress by making bound buttonholes as illustrated, and make loop buttons by sewing a self-covered button to each end of a piece of braid or cord that is just long enough to reach from one buttonhole to the one on the opposite side. This arrangement will hold the edges of the dress together without overlapping them.

Model 21D.—Made entirely of one kind of material and with no trimming other than a few buttonholed bars that are used for finishing the back darts, this model depends entirely on the novelty of its lines for success. That such dependence is entirely justifiable can be proved by no better evidence than the dignity and charm that are decidedly a part of the design. Poiret twill in navy blue is the fabric employed, 4½ yards of this being required for the average figure.

This model, because of its long lines, is particularly adapted to the stout woman and merely requires any slight change that may be needed in the collar to make it individually becoming. For the majority of stout women, a much less decided flare and a narrower effect through the upper portion are desirable.

A one-piece dress pattern that hangs on practically straight lines may be used for cutting this model. Outline on this pattern the side overdress sections. Then cut on the marked lines and place the front and back portions so that the under-arm seams meet at the hip line and are separated 2 or 3 inches at the lower edge. Then, to provide additional flare, slash both the front and back portions through the center, lengthwise, from the lower edge almost to the hip line, and separate these 2 or 3 inches at the lower edge. Cut the side sections in one piece, and join these to the front and back sections after the under-arm seam of these sections has been stitched. Finish the corners of the front and back sections by applying a facing of silk and forming tailored corners according to the instructions given in *Tailored and Lingerie Blouses*, Part 2.

In joining the side sections, first turn under the edge of the upper portion, which is just above the natural hip line, baste this turned edge over the corresponding edge of the lower section, and stitch on the basted line. Then baste the side lengthwise edges together in preparation for stitching a plain seam. After stitching the seam, turn and press the edges back on the front and back sections in order to emphasize the panel effects, making them appear as if applied over the side sections.

In order to curve the dress in a trifle at the back waist line, form darts at the points illustrated, and to make these darts more ornamental in character, finish them with buttonholed bars worked with buttonhole twist in practically the same manner as the bar used at the end of a regulation buttonhole.

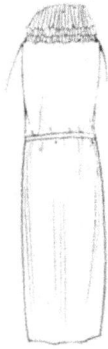

21 B

21 A

21 D

21 C

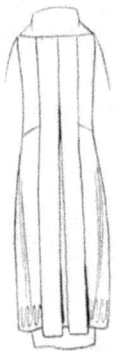

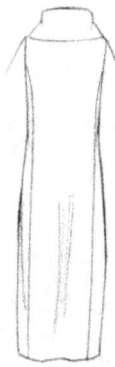

Suits and Wraps

Model 22A.—Some seasons we hear that Paris is not giving a thought to the tailored suit, hence that it will not be worn. Though Paris does dictate a goodly part of our fashions, she will never be able successfully to extricate the tailored suit from the wardrobe of the American woman. It has become a factor, especially with the business woman, who finds it unusually becoming, comfortable, and practical.

Of all types of tailored suits, the one strictly tailored and built on long, mannish lines is the most favored. Not that the very same style of suit continues in vogue from one season to another, for subtle changes, such as slight variance in the width of the collar and revers, the length of the shoulder line, the fitting of the sleeve, and the length of the jacket, or the more noticeable difference of the manner of closing or the trimming employed, proclaim a suit as up to the minute in detail or as decidedly of a past season's type.

At the present time, jacket lengths vary according to the style. Most of the suits that are built on mannish lines are of considerably more than finger length, while those of the more youthful box or flare types are made hip length or shorter.

This model of navy tricotine, which is of the mannish tailored type, is an excellent style for the large-proportioned woman. The closing, which is effected by means of loop buttons, the trimming of bias bands of self-material, and the straight gathered skirt with diagonal pockets at each side front are features typical of the showing of suits for spring.

In developing this suit for the average figure, you will need 3½ yards of 54-inch fabric and 2¾ yards of 36- or 40-inch plain-colored silk for lining. Use a semifitting foundation coat pattern for cutting the jacket, arranging the center- and side-front pattern sections on the material so that they meet from the point where you wish to place the lower pocket to the lower edge of the pattern and thus permit the lower portion to be cut without a seam and the shaping of the upper portion to be accomplished by the dart that extends from the lower pocket to the center of the shoulder.

For interlining, use very soft light-weight canvas or cambric in the shoulder and bust portions, as well as along the edges where it is generally employed. Turn the edges of the bias strips and slip-stitch them in position along both edges.

Model 22B.—Chinese influence is very noticeable in the youthful spring suit models, of which this is a very representative type. And the sash? This, also, is truly representative, for the suit without it has a very serious time trying to appear at all swagger in this season of colorful and voluminous sashes of every description and for every purpose.

Piquetine in pagoda blue, which is a dark shade with an ever-so-slight suggestion of green, is the material used for the suit, 3 yards of this fabric being required. The sash is of henna-colored satin with wide, silk-fringed ends, 1¼ yards of satin and ⅜ yard of fringe being needed for this. For lining, 2½ yards of silk 36 inches wide or 2 yards 40 inches in width will be sufficient. This may be of a color to match the sash; otherwise, of some neutral color that is harmonious with it.

Cut out the jacket with the aid of a kimono coat pattern that is moderately flared in the body portion as well as the sleeve. In developing this style, the use of soft interlining is unnecessary except in the collar and around the edges.

Model 22C.—Rose-color and white flannel comply in every respect with Fashion's mandates in this sports suit with its unlined Tuxedo jacket, roomy patch pockets, and knife-plaited skirt that gives a suggestion of the use of striped material. Of the rose color, 3 yards of 54-inch fabric will be required, and of the white, 2⅛ yards of this same width.

Make the skirt of twelve straight strips of material 8 or 9 inches wide, six of each color. Join these strips with plain seams; then press the seam edges together to one side and, in making the plaits, see that each of the seams forms the inner edge of the plait of one color that overlaps the contrasting color. In the jacket, make plain seams, press them open, and bind them.

Model 22D.—Coats, in the ordinary sense of the term, have had a very real struggle for existence since the dominance of wraps and capes has become so pronounced. But even while this vogue for wraps is at its height, the person who wishes a coat of practical nature for all sorts of wear and perhaps for several seasons' use can do no better than shun the wrap models and select a coat conservative in design but, withal, of a style that is in no sense ordinary.

Such qualifications are met in this model of very fine velour in a rather deep shade of gray. The large roomy collar, wide sleeves, deep kimono armhole, and loose-fitting effect make the coat an unusually comfortable style and one especially good for wear over light summer dresses. The trimming bands are of bias self-material and are finished at the lower end with arrowheads worked with gray buttonhole twist. About 3½ yards of 54-inch fabric is required for this model. The coat may be lined throughout, or the lining entirely omitted. Of lining material 36 inches wide, 3¾ yards will be required.

Cut the coat with the aid of a kimono coat pattern made with a very deep armhole. In trying out a muslin model, you will probably find that the placing of a horizontal dart at the front waist line will permit the coat to be cut on a more nearly straight line at the lower edge and prevent it from falling toward the front. Form the collar pattern, also, by experimenting with muslin, rolling it as high as you desire and shaping it to produce the effect that is illustrated.

Model 22E.—Capes and wraps are following so many extremes in regard to styles, fabrics, and trimmings that there seems to be no purpose that they overlook. For utility wear, there are the most serviceable styles and materials imaginable; then there are the in-between types, and, at the other extreme, wraps of lace, net, or chiffon of the most exquisite, even though perishable, nature. The silk wrap is the fad of the moment. If of taffeta, it is smartest when made of black in ruffled cape styles; of satin, it is favored in black, also, and while its style ranges from cape to near-coat models, it is almost invariably blistered or quilted; of crêpe de Chine or the heavier crêpe fabrics, it is found in the seasonal range of colors and depends largely on embroidery for trimming.

This last type of wrap is an especially good one for woolen fabrics also, as is evidenced by this model of suède cloth in a deep colorful tan with wool embroidery slightly lighter in tone. It is not advisable to use material less than 54 inches wide for this style, as narrower material would necessitate seam lines that would mar the attractiveness of the design. Of material 54 inches wide, 3¼ yards will prove sufficient. For lining, 4 yards of 36-inch silk will be required, and for the embroidery, 18 skeins of wool.

A muslin-modeled pattern is necessary for cutting this design. Make this with a lengthwise thread at the center front and center back, and, by means of a vertical dart at the side back and a horizontal seam line at the front, make the material fit smoothly over the shoulders.

The collar of this wrap, which is extended to form the front trimming bands, should also be modeled in muslin. Let the straight of the material extend along the fronts, shape the collar around the neck line, and pin a bias seam at the center back. Make the sleeve trimming bands of straight strips.

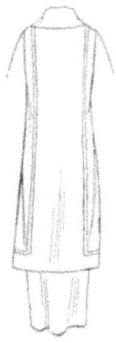

22 A

22 B

22 C

22 D

Children's Dresses

Regardless of how much one's elders talk about the charm and beauty of the styles of our grandmothers, one cannot have a great deal of respect for old-time designers. Quite startling, yes, but certainly justifiable unless history and preserved fashion plates are not considered reliable sources of information as to the sort of apparel little ladies were forced to wear many decades ago. Tight bodices and long and voluminously full and "fussy" skirts were perhaps all right for grown-ups and for very prim little maidens who sat all day and made cross-stitch samplers or knitted tidies.

But surely there was another type of child—one so in advance of her time that she loved nothing better than to romp and play in the open, to make mud pies, and to climb trees and fences. Just think of the "indignities" to which she submitted that demure frock of hers! Or, better still, try to imagine her feelings of delight and amazement had she been translated into modern times and permitted to wear the kind of clothes that Fashion is now sanctioning for children. A mere thought of that little old-fashioned girl's frocks is sufficient to make one shout for joy because of the privilege of owning a goodly supply of modern dresses, easy fitting, short, and, best of all, *wearable*.

Even with the very practical nature of children's styles, daintiness and attractiveness have not been sacrificed to any extent, for there are dresses of all kinds of materials made in all sorts of ways, each according to the purpose for which it is intended. For play and school, there are frocks of gingham, chambray, ratine, satine, cotton poplin, and Japanese crêpe; for dress-up wear, of such lovely materials as tissue, dimity, organdie, net, dotted Swiss, crêpe de Chine, Georgette crêpe, and taffeta; then, for either school or dress-up wear in early spring, of pongee, challis, serge, and tricotine.

Fabric trimmings seem to be in greater abundance than any other kind. Most often the fabric is used as a binding, but it has many other odd uses, such as pointed effects, tabs, ruffles, and appliqué motifs. Embroidery, lace, and buttons, especially those of novel pearl variety, are also prominent as trimmings.

Colors for children are quite similar to those suggested for women, with the brighter and more youthful shades, of course, predominating. A great deal of attention is given to lilac, green, and orange, all of which are rather unusual.

Model 23.—A very practical dress is ever the first consideration of the average mother. This model is all that can be desired, not only in regard to its practical nature, but also because of its rather severe smartness. The material is chambray of apricot color, the bindings and collar are of white organdie or fine piqué, and the inserted trimming in the collar is fine rickrack braid.

For a girl of ten, 3 yards of chambray, ½ yard of organdie, and 1¾ yards of rickrack braid are required for this style.

You may cut the waist and skirt in one piece, using a plain one-piece dress pattern as a guide, or, if you prefer, you may cut the skirt separate, making it, in this instance, of two straight strips of material each 24 to 28 inches wide and of a length that will permit of at least a 3-inch hem. The advisability of providing wide hems is not overlooked by the far-sighted mother, for she realizes that the prolonged use of the garment is usually dependent on its permitting of a change in the length.

For each of the tunic portions, cut a straight section of material 3 or 4 inches wider than the underskirt sections and long enough to reach to within 2 inches of the lower edge of the skirt. Bind the sides and lower edges of these sections; then, in applying them to the waist line, leave about 6 inches of the upper edge near the sides free so that it extends out in loop effect. Then cut the upper edge of the loops on a slightly curved line, as the illustration shows, and bind these edges also.

Cut the organdie collar and cuffs to extend merely to the rickrack. Finish the edge of each with a tiny rolled or flat hem, and secure the rickrack to this hem. For the outer portion of the collar and cuffs, cut bias strips about 1¼ inches wide, fold these through the center lengthwise, and then turn the raw edges to the inside of the strip and fit the strip carefully around the rickrack, securing the rickrack to it and stretching the outer edge of the bias in order to adjust it to the curved portions. Miter the bias strip to form each corner of the cuffs.

Model 23A.—Spring satines are of such a fine, glossy character that at first glance they appear to be satin. This appearance alone is sufficient to win popular favor, but when, in addition, the "tubbing" quality of satine is considered, the wise mother will add at least one satine frock to the summer wardrobe of each little miss in her home.

One of the most attractive as well as most favored colors in satine is a rather yellowish orange, the color chosen for this model. A medium-bright shade of blue is the most effective color for trimming; sometimes this is employed for embroidery and bindings, as in this model; other times it is used for appliqué motifs of the same fabric or even of leather.

White dotted Swiss is the fabric of the blouse or guimpe of this little style. Blue satine bindings, like those used to finish the edges of the straps of the dress, are applied to the sleeve and frill edges of the guimpe.

Made for a girl of ten, the design requires 2 yards of satine, 1¼ yards of dotted Swiss, and 3 skeins of cotton or wool floss.

Chambray, linen, or gingham might also be used for this frock. If a very plain style is desired, the strap waist may be faced rather than bound, the embroidery omitted, and the guimpe made of white lawn or dimity with a Peter Pan collar.

Model 23B.—Big events in one's life, such as graduating from grammar school, taking part in a May-Day festival, or being a bride's youthful attendant, require a costume befitting one's position of importance. If one happens to be initiating one's teens, a frock modeled on grown-up lines is the safest selection, and if this same frock happens to be of net, it gives an added suggestion of dignity that is very satisfactory.

Six straight, "flying" panels, picot-edged and trimmed with square motifs formed by overlapping rows of shirred satin ribbon, add character to the straight double-net skirt. Three similar ribbon trimming motifs are applied to the plain, gathered waist, and a double collar of net, lace-edged, provides the finish at the neck. The sash is of 6-inch satin ribbon.

For a miss of twelve, 2 yards of net 2 yards wide will prove ample to cut the skirt double and to make a waist lining as well as the blouse and sleeves. In addition, 2¼ yards of lace, 20 yards of ¾-inch ribbon, and 3 yards of sash ribbon are required. If desired, lace may be substituted for the ribbon motifs in order to make the dress less expensive.

Make the panels of this dress about 6 inches wide. Form the collar pattern by experimenting with muslin.

To make the ribbon motifs, gather one edge of the ribbon on the sewing machine, making the gathering only slightly full. Then baste the net to a piece of tissue or light-weight paper so as to give it sufficient body and baste the ribbon in position, starting at the center to form the square motifs. In forming the corners, hold the ribbon sufficiently full to make an absolutely square finish. After basting the ribbon, stitch on the basted line through the paper as well as the net and then tear the paper away. In stitching net seams or in applying lace to net, you will find it helpful to hold paper underneath the line on which the stitching is to be done, for this will prevent the net from being drawn under the needle plate of the sewing machine.

Model 23

23 A

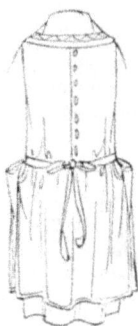

23 B

Designs for Children

Model 23C.—Until a season or so ago, the shades ranging from lavender to violet were generally classed as "grandmother" colors. Just why it was left for modern designers to sanction their use for children is a mystery; certainly, not because grandmothers were reluctant to sacrifice monopoly of these colors, for a grandmother is the last person in the world we can accuse of selfishness. At any rate, to be strictly in accord with Fashion's dictates this spring, every wee girl's wardrobe must boast of at least one frock of violet hue, provided, of course, the wee girl's type indicates that such a color is becoming to her.

In this model, lilac-and-white checked gingham relies on a deeper violet tone for its trimming of cross-stitching. The fulness in the waist portion is held in with smocking-stitches, which are used as a foundation for the cross-stitching. The collar and cuffs are of a finely ribbed quality of white piqué.

For a little girl of six, provide about 2 yards of material, ¼ yard of piqué or linen for collar and cuffs, and 3 or 4 skeins of floss for the cross-stitching. Cut the dress with the aid of a plain one-piece pattern, slashing this lengthwise and separating the pieces to provide the fulness.

Model 23D.—Regardless of the attractive and unusual colors that each season introduces, the white dress never loses its charm. Besides, it has real utility value, for there are any number of occasions that call for a white frock, and not to have one on hand might mean the loss of an opportunity for service and enjoyment.

Georgette crêpe is the very nicest material that can be used for a model such as this, because the sheerness and softness of the fabric permit of tucks that appear neither heavy nor bunglesome. The separation of the wide tucks by narrow ones is a feature evident in many models. The sash may be of ribbon in just the prettiest color a little mind can conceive, or it may be of white, provided no touch of color is desired in the dress. Provide 2¾ yards of Georgette crêpe and 2½ yards of ribbon for the average child of eight.

Fabrics other than Georgette crêpe, which are suitable for this model, are fine crêpe de Chine, batiste, organdie, and dotted Swiss. The tucks may be secured by machine hemstitching in a color to match the sash.

No pattern is required for the skirt. Simply provide two lengths of material that will give the skirt width you desire and that will provide sufficient material for the tucks. In order to make a correct estimate of the amount that will be required for tucks, decide just how wide the tucks must be to make the spacings attractive and the uppermost tuck as close to the waist line as illustrated.

For the waist, use a plain kimono-waist pattern and outline on it the low, round neck line and the panel effect. Cut the underwaist without fulness at the neck line. To provide fulness in the neck line of the panel pattern, make vertical slashes at two points between the center front and the shoulder and separate these slashes ½ inch or so merely at the neck line. In cutting the panel, provide the extra length required for the tucks by making allowance below the waist line.

Model 23E.—If any proof is desired that the popularity of checked gingham will be as marked as has been predicted, it may be had in the silks that are woven in imitation of gingham patterns. Such a silk is the material used for this little dress of blue-and-white check. The shell trimming is of plain blue ribbon applied in pointed motifs.

For only occasional or dress-up wear should silk be selected, for the design is very plain and suggestive of the use of less expensive materials. Checked gingham may, of course, be used with good effect, and plain colored fabrics with trimming of the same material in contrasting color would be attractive.

For the average child of eight, about 3 yards of material will be required. For trimming, 5 yards of 1-inch ribbon or ½ yard of contrasting material must be provided.

No patterns other than a plain waist and a sleeve pattern are needed for the cutting of the dress as the skirt is made simply of two lengths of material.

To make the shell trimming of ribbon, cut the ribbon into strips that are ½ inch longer than twice its width. Then, with the wrong side of the strip uppermost, fold the lower corners up so that the finished edges meet at the center and are even with a crosswise thread of the ribbon, thus forming the triangular effect illustrated. Press the folds with an iron so as to hold them in position. In applying the shell trimming, fold over the finished edge the ends that extend beyond it and baste the shells flat in a continuous row, as illustrated; then stitch directly on the turned edge and trim away the raw edges that are evident. Instructions for making the shell trimming of strips of material are given in *Dresses,* Part 1.

Model 23F.—One of the most treasured possessions of the wee girl is her party frock, for with it are linked memories of many a good time, as well as anticipation of happy events to come. A party dress is particularly dear to her heart if its initial appearance was on some especially momentous occasion, such as a wedding at which she acted as flower girl. And if her flower-girl costume happens to be of peach-colored taffeta, ruffled and short, with ruffled bloomers of the same material peeping below the skirt hem, what more is needed for perfection?

If worn as a flower-girl costume, this little frock may be accompanied by a hat made of the same material in a poke shape with a plaited brim and corded crown and trimmed with blue velvet ribbon and pink and yellow roses.

For a six-year-old tot of average size, 3½ yards of material will be required for the dress, the bloomers, and the frills. In addition, 1 yard of material is needed for the hat.

A style of this kind might be developed in satine for more ordinary wear; or, with the bloomers omitted, the little frock might be made of organdie or of dotted Swiss with organdie ruffles machine-hemstitched to secure them in position.

A plain kimono-waist pattern on which the abbreviated sleeve length is marked should be used for cutting the bodice of this dress. Before having the ruffles plaited, have one edge picoted. Then, in applying the ruffles to the skirt and bloomers, secure the edge in a very narrow tuck or French-seam effect.

Model 23G.—In general, coat styles for children are developed along slightly "wrappy" lines, but while this style predominates, there are coats of the straight-line regulation style, others of extremely flaring lines, and capes of taffeta or of wool, quite similar to those that were popular last season. Coat fabrics include serge, tricotine, piquetine, covert cloth, homespuns, Bolivia, and other light and medium-weight woolens.

Embroidery does not play an extremely important part in the trimming of coats for children, but applied in moderate degree and a tasteful manner, as in this style, it adds very distinctive touches to coats of "dress-up" character. The material of this model is soft cloth in a colorful tan, with embroidery and fringe ends in blue. The fulness at the back may be merely gathered or smocked with self-color.

Taffeta is an excellent material to use for a coat of this kind, provided it is intended for only occasional wear. But the style is of such a nature that, made of dark-colored wool without the embroidery, a very practical coat would result.

The coat may be made with or without a lining, as preferred. The cuffs are of straight strips of material embroidered and then faced with light-weight or self-material. The collar may be faced with the same material as the cuffs.

23 G

23 C

23 D

23 E

23 F

Magic Pattern: *Circular Apron*

▶▶▶ THIS DESIGN is ideal for rayon taffeta or organdie. Decorate it with bows, flowers, or pockets.

It requires ¾ yd. of 36- to 40-in. fabric.

Measure down on the selvage 4½ in., clip selvage, and tear or cut off this crosswise strip to make your waist band (A in diagram). Fold apron piece through center lengthwise and pin selvages together.

Measure along fold to a depth of one-fourth waist measurement plus 1 in. to locate B. Measure up from fold one-third of the waist measurement, plus 2 in. (C).

Draw curve B to C. To do this, tie a string to a pencil, place pencil at B; then about 2 in. beyond edge of fabric hold other end of string (D). Make curve by swinging pencil from B to C. Draw similar curve from E to F, testing correctness of second curve by a practice swing or two to find the correct point at which to hold string.

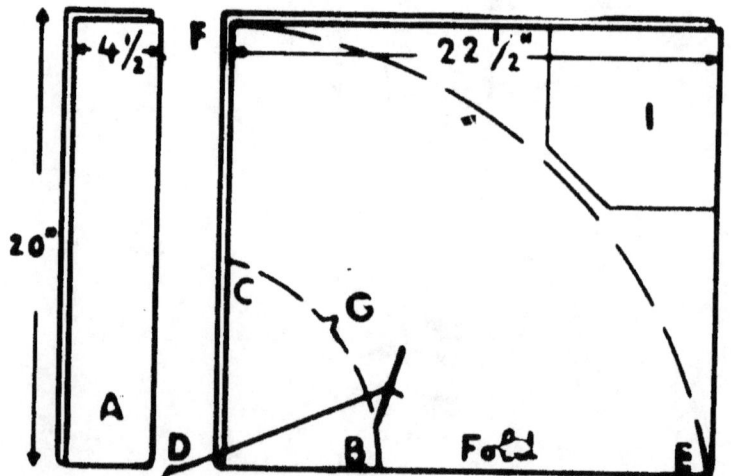

When narrower fabric is used, the distance from C to F will be narrower. Cut on curved lines for waistline and bottom edge.

Make notch G 6 in. from C. Make a line of gathers from G to B on both sides of apron, using a long machine stitch.

Draw up bobbin thread so that shirring measures 4 in. Make ¼-in. hem on side and bottom edges.

Center band at center of waistline, right sides together. Pin and stitch from one side of apron to the other.

Fold one tie end in half, wrong side out, and stitch edges together and across ends, stitching from G to H as in detail. Repeat with other tie end. Turn tie ends inside out. Turn under raw edge of band and whip.

Piece I can be used for pockets.

Your Measurement Chart & Notes on Making Magic Patterns

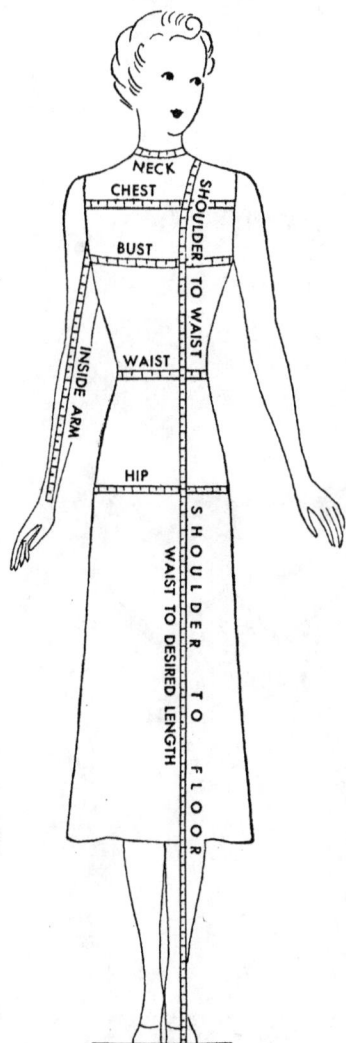

BUST (Fullest Part)............._____

WAIST ...._____

HIP (Fullest Part) ...._____

WIDTH OF CHEST..........._____

FRONT WAIST LENGTH
Shoulder to Waist............._____

FRONT SKIRT LENGTH
Waist to Desired Length........._____

FRONT FULL LENGTH
Shoulder to Floor ...._____

NECK (At Base) ...._____

SHOULDER
Neck to Armhole Line..........._____

ARMHOLE ...._____

WIDTH OF BACK ...._____

BACK LENGTH
Neck to Waist ...._____

BACK LENGTH
Neck to Floor................._____

OUTSIDE ARM
Shoulder to Wrist (Arm Bent)...._____

INSIDE ARM
Armhole to Wrist (Arm Straight)..._____

UPPER ARM (Fullest Part)......._____

ELBOW (Arm Bent) ...._____

WRIST ...._____

HAND (Closed) ...._____

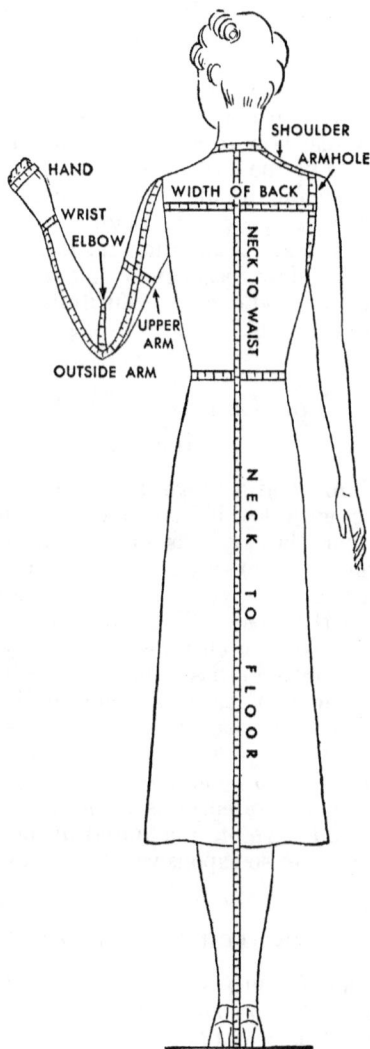

Keep Accurate Measurements

Since the garments in this book are all cut from measurements, it is necessary to have accurate ones to follow. Keep a list of your own measurements always at hand for ready reference.

Measurements for fitted garments should be taken over the type of foundation garments you expect to wear with them. Remove dress, jacket, or coat, which would distort the measurements. Do not take measurements too tight. Make all easy enough for comfort. The chart shows how to place the tape correctly for each measurement.

Making The Pattern

If you have the least doubt about your ability to chalk out the garment on your fabric, then rough it out first with crayon or heavy pencil on wrapping paper or newspaper. Cut out the paper pattern and use it to cut your garment. Cutting from a diagram, you can be sure that the proportions are correct for your size and that the garment will be a good fit.

You Can Make the Loveliest Linens, Curtains, Draperies and Pillows

DO not think that through the Institute Course you learn only to make clothes. No, indeed. You learn not only to make every type of garment, but to do every other kind of sewing and needlework as well. In fact, the Course is so complete that no matter what you may want to make for yourself or for your home, if it can be made with needle and thread and materials, you will know just how to create it with your own hands at a mere fraction of the cost to buy it.

Have you any idea how much money you spend unnecessarily every year on household accessories? Your curtains, bureau scarfs, table runners, table cloths, napkins, towels, sheets, pillow cases, even your heavy draperies and hangings, all these can be beautifully made at home at a substantial saving.

You Can Have Pretty New Curtains for Every Room

Think what a delight it will be to be able to beautify your home with lovely hangings—gay chintzes or dimity for summer—heavy silks or velvets, for winter. And your curtains! You will no longer have to keep on making your old curtains do, year after year. Now, in a very short time, and at the most trifling expenditure, you can learn to make all kinds of new curtains, whenever you want them—dainty, frilled, dotted swiss or point d'esprit ones for the bedroom, pretty ones of scrim or voile for the children's room, with perhaps some charming little designs embroidered in colored worsted or appliquéd on with bits of colored cotton scraps. You will even be able to make exquisite casement curtains or French door curtains, for living or dining room—the kind that you have often admired in the homes of your friends and yet are so expensive when you purchase them outright.

Now You Can Afford Lovely Linens

And of course you can make all your own bed coverings and table linens. Formerly expensive materials were thought necessary, but now the preference is for those beautifully made and finished, those that show good taste and harmonize perfectly in color and design with their surroundings. By hemstitching or embroidering them yourself, you can, without paying a cent for anything but the material, make for yourself the handsomest household linens that can be procured anywhere.

And if you wish to make money on your work, this is one of the most profitable ways of doing it. There is always a demand for beautifully monogrammed, scalloped, hand-hemstitched, lace-edged or otherwise hand-decorated household linens, and the hand work on these makes them very valuable and they always command the very highest prices. Indeed, this kind of hand work is the most profitable kind of needlework, for, without any expenditure on your part at all, except for needles and thread, it increases the value of the material three, five, and often tenfold.

Originally published in "How You Can Have More and Prettier Clothes" Book, 1925

Gives You a Splendid Independent Means of Earning Money at Home

THOUSANDS of women are confronted with the problem, "How shall I provide a living for my family and myself?" Thousands more must choose some vocation because they must help with family expenses, and numberless others want to know the joy of being independent and having a good income of their own.

To the woman or girl in any of these circumstances there is no work more enjoyable or profitable than dressmaking. Formerly it was difficult to prepare for success in this field, for it was necessary either to become an apprentice in a shop or to attend a resident school. Most women have neither the time nor the money to leave home to learn dressmaking by these methods and too often there are little ones dependent upon them as well. But now through the Woman's Institute the way is open for any woman to fit herself right in her own home, without interrupting her daily duties, to become financially successful and independent as a dressmaker.

You know from experience in your own community that good dressmakers are always in demand. Even those who do only plain sewing are always busy, while those with the ability to design clothes of distinction for their customers command high prices and are always engaged for months ahead.

There are many women in every community too busy in other professions to make their own clothes and many women of wealth who prefer to have their garments made by an expert. These women are accustomed to paying good prices.

Widow Earns $95 Quickly

An Institute member in Pennsylvania, suddenly left a widow, tells how the Institute helped her: "In October I was suddenly confronted with the fact that I had to support myself and three children. I was at my wits' end as to how I would be able to keep my little family together. Then one day I read about the Woman's Institute and took up dressmaking. I have earned $95 making dresses for women of my town in the last few weeks and have all the work ahead that I can do."

The Joy of Independence

What a pleasure and satisfaction it is to know that you have a profession of your own, that you possess a skill by which others seek to benefit. As a dressmaker, you will be independent for all time. You will have no further worries about losing your position, no fears of the day when you may be thrown on your own resources. You will be free to set your own hours, to take vacations and enjoy the pleasures of life as you desire. You will know what it really means to be independent.

A member in a small town in Minnesota who has established a shop in her own home writes to tell of her success and then says: "Best of all I have been able to take the first real vacation in ten years—three weeks without a care and with plenty of money for needed clothes and to have a good time. And I feel I owe it all to the Institute who made it possible for me to learn dressmaking."

Moreover, you can earn while you are learning. Very soon after starting you will be able to do plain sewing, to make blouses, simple dresses, and lingerie, and you can command good wages for your work.

A member in Idaho writes: "I have made over $200 since commencing the course and I have the name of being our best dressmaker, although I have taken only a small part of the course."

As you proceed with your course, your skill will increase, your knowledge of the work will broaden, and you will be able to steadily increase the price of your services. So by the time you have completed your course, you should have earned its cost several times over. There is scarcely another profession in which this would be possible.

Originally published in "How You Can Have More and Prettier Clothes" Book, 1925

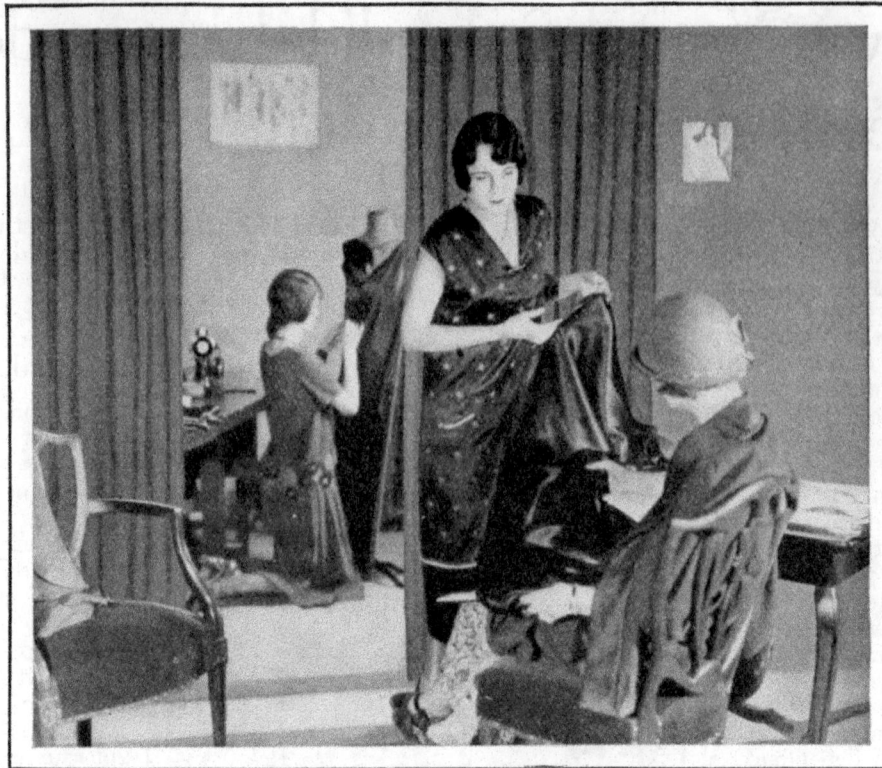

You Can Have a Dressmaking Shop of Your Own

SUCCESS comes sure and soon to the skilled dressmaker, and it is so easy to get started. There are several ways to begin.

You may, if you wish, start in your own home by doing work for your immediate friends and through their recommendations add an ever widening circle of customers.

Or you can for a time secure a position in some dressmaking establishment. You will be certain to receive at least fairly good wages and your advancement should be rapid.

Or you can establish a shop of your own. This will be a venture in which you can take real pride. Little or no capital will be needed at the start. As you develop greater skill and your reputation for doing good work becomes known, your patronage will increase. You can enlarge your establishment as the business grows.

A widow in New York State says: "I made an average of $40 a month just in spare time the first year; then I moved to Main Street and turned one side of my house into a shop. The first month I made $72, the second $90, and I am going to keep right on going ahead."

The Institute will give you complete directions as to how to open your dressmaking shop. It will tell you what equipment you will need and give the fullest and most explicit instructions on the best methods of developing a successful business that you may well be proud of.

A Massachusetts student who has opened a shop writes: "I have several working for me. I expected the work to come in slowly, but I sent out one hundred engraved cards and the next day had eight customers here with work. Does it not speak well for the gowns your course helped me make for myself—that they came flocking to my little gown shop? My work has brought in over $500 in two months and a half above expenses, and I have thirty-five gowns to finish."

There is absolutely no question about your attaining professional skill through our courses. The lessons are thorough and complete, yet marvelously clear and simple. Their study is so fascinating you will wonder why you did not begin sooner. The entire course covers every principle, every possible detail you will need to know. When you have completed it, you will be able to handle any kind of work that comes to you, to make anything from a blouse to an elaborate evening gown, to originate and design unusual charming styles, to fit any type of figure, and to command your own price for your time and knowledge.

Originally published in "How You Can Have More and Prettier Clothes" Book, 1925

The Simplicity of This New Way
Makes Dressmaking a Pleasure

YOU will be surprised and delighted when you find how easy and fascinating it is to learn to make clothes by the Institute's new method of teaching.

In the first place, you learn by doing. You learn to make an apron by making an apron. You learn to make a dress by making a dress.

All the usual tedious preliminaries have been eliminated. You begin almost at once on the actual creation of the clothes you would like to have. With your very first instruction book you receive materials for a pretty garment and full directions for making it.

So in just a few hours after receiving your first big interesting package from the Institute, you actually have something pretty to wear.

But this is only the beginning. In your second lesson you learn to make seven different types of garments without the use of patterns.

So step by step as you proceed, you learn to make smart one-piece dresses, blouses, skirts, dainty lingerie, and children's clothes, afternoon and evening clothes, and tailored coats and wraps, in fact you learn through these easy fascinating lessons to make every kind of garment required to be becomingly and distinctively dressed.

Every Step of Fascinating Interest

That is one secret of the remarkable success of this new method. You are always planning and making something interesting and fascinating, always fashioning with your own hands some dainty attractive garment that you have longed to have. There are no dull, tiring moments. You will become so enthusiastic and delighted with your new accomplishment that you will want to spend every spare minute creating pretty things to wear.

All through the course, the work is so arranged that each lesson makes the next one easy. You are never asked to do something for which you have not been fully prepared. Each lesson carries you another step forward so when you reach some undertaking you had always thought difficult you find that it is not difficult at all.

Woman's Institute instruction books are different from any you have ever seen in a school-room. They have been written especially for study at home. They tell everything that it is essential to know about each subject in such simple language that you cannot fail to understand.

Pictures Make Everything Clear

Then each book is profusely illustrated with step-by-step pictures showing just what to do. They are so clear and distinct that you can see every stitch and fold as plainly as though you had the garment itself in your own hands. One student wrote that she could almost learn dressmaking from the pictures alone.

Always you will have some of these tempting books at hand so interesting that you will be impatient to start the lovely garments they teach you to make. Always there will be intimate, friendly letters of commendation and help coming from members of The Institute Staff. Then four times a year your beautiful copy of "Fashion Service," the most complete and practical of all fashion books, and every month will come the friendly visit of "Inspiration," brimful of ideas, fashion notes, sewing helps—your own magazine.

In fact, from the very day you enroll with the Institute you will find that learning dressmaking and designing by this new plan is a delightful experience, so interesting and thoroughly enjoyable that you will wonder why you ever thought there was anything difficult or uninteresting about it.

Originally published in "How You Can Have More and Prettier Clothes" Book, 1925

These Two Wonderful Publications Will Bring Frequent Friendly Help

As soon as you join the Institute it will be our purpose and privilege to *constantly* help you to plan and make lovely clothes.   So as a part of your instruction service you will receive four times a year our Quarterly Fashion Service, presenting the very newest styles of the current season, and every month you will receive the delightful and practical magazine "Inspiration."   Both are prepared and published by the Institute especially for Institute students.

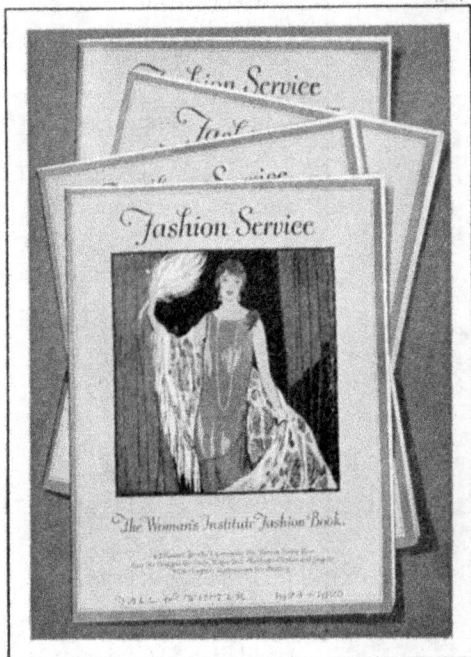

Fashion Service—Quarterly

FASHION SERVICE is distinctive from all other fashion publications.   Four times a year it will come to you—on the 10th of February, May, September and November—bringing the correct answer to each season's questions—the right silhouette, the right colors, the right fabrics, the right skirt length, the right waist line, the right neck line, the right trimmings.   But far more than that, it brings you plans for your complete wardrobe, the choicest selections from the season's fashions, and best of all, complete instructions for making everything.   This makes it the most practical of all sources of fashion information.   Thousands of students plan and make all their clothes from it each season.

Fashion Service is handsomely printed and generous in size, at least 48 pages with covers in four colors, 12 or more pages of fashion drawings in color, many pages of wonderful photographs of dresses planned and made in our own dressmaking department.   Altogether each issue contains more than 100 designs of dresses, suits, wraps, hats, lingerie and children's clothes—with full instructions for making.

Inspiration—Every Month

"Inspiration"—the Institute's own monthly magazine —is indeed an inspiration to the thousands of women who read it eagerly, from cover to cover, every month.   For it is *exactly* the kind of magazine that women want.   Without being bulky and unwieldy, it is brimming with *practical* information about just the things women want to know.

The monthly visits of Inspiration will always be helpful, for the editors have a perfect understanding of just the help our students need.   There are lovely illustrated pages giving up-to-the-minute information about clothes and millinery.   Then there are new kinds of dishes to prepare, new and delightful ways of spending vacations, new kinds of profitable work to do, hints on clubs and club programs, slenderizing fashions, and dozens of other topics equally dear to the feminine heart.   And these matters are all discussed in an intimate, friendly, common sense way, with an aim to practical, usefulness.

"Inspiration" is a looked-for, welcome visitor to every student's home and brings a monthly message of cheer that makes your Institute membership all the more delightful.

Originally published in "How You Can Have More and Prettier Clothes" Book, 1925

What You Will Receive When You Enroll

TAKING up this course is going to be one of the most important events in your life, for it is going to bring you more real happiness and satisfaction, win for you more admiration and save you more money than anything you have ever done. So we want you to know exactly what is going to happen when you start.

Immediately you send us your application, you will be enrolled as a regular member of the Woman's Institute for the course you have selected and within a few days your first packages of supplies will be delivered to your door. They will bring you:

First—You will receive the first three fascinating instruction books of your course, containing instructions so simple and easy to follow that you will at last realize that sewing and dressmaking have a fascination you never dreamed possible.

Second—You will receive a copy of the handsome 250-page cloth-bound first volume of your Reference Library, "Sewing Materials," the most practical guide ever published for the selection and use of fabrics of all kinds.

Third—The handsome big current issue of Fashion Service—the Institute's own fashion book —containing 50 or more designs for smart, modish dresses with the simplest possible instructions for making, also dozens of designs for wraps, suits, hats, lingerie, and children's clothes with directions for making each one.

Fourth—A great variety of supplies to help you get started and full instructions for making the most rapid progress in learning the whole delightful art of dressmaking.

And this will only be the beginning, for there will be fifteen other fascinating instruction books to follow, and three more of the large cloth-bound volumes of your Reference Library all coming to you in more and more packages as you proceed with your work, and Fashion Service four times a year and Inspiration every month—all bringing you the simplest possible instructions for making lovely clothes of every type.

And then the feature that makes the course personal to your own needs—the constant individual guidance of our expert instructors and their personal sympathetic help on every clothes problem about which you may write. Their letters to you will be a positive inspiration. They find their greatest joy in helping women and girls to have the lovely, attractive clothes that can mean so much in their lives and they will help you in the warm, understanding, personal way that they would if they were right beside you in your own home.

And Now—Let's Take the First Step

HERE in this book you have the full story of just how you learn and what you learn through this interesting practical plan. Now that you have read it and have learned how easy and fascinating the making of beautiful clothes can be by this method, you are ready to take the first step.

It matters not how much or how little experience you may have had, you will find here exactly the help and training you need. Whatever your circumstances you can now have an abundance of pretty clothes at a mere fraction of what they would otherwise cost. And you can give them that style and distinctiveness that will insure your success as a dressmaker if you wish to use your skill professionally.

Can you imagine the sheer joy of having all the lovely clothes you want at almost unbelievable savings—or the satisfaction of having a pleasant and profitable profession? Then let us help you turn this desire into an actual and glorious reality.

And now let us take the first step. Fill out and mail your application and get started at once on one of the most delightful and profitable experiences you have ever had.

WOMAN'S INSTITUTE
Scranton, Pa.

Originally published in "How You Can Have More and Prettier Clothes" Book, 1925

The Best Investment You Ever Made

Saves Cost in One Month

In one month I have earned all that my course will cost me.
GRACE L. HOGAN,
Dorchester, Mass.

Saves Cost Twice Over

With only half of my course finished I have saved twice its cost.
MISS BONNIE CONGLETON,
Clearwater Lake, Wis.

Saves $100 on Five Lessons

I am perfectly safe in saying I have saved at least $100.00 on my first five lessons.
MRS. LEA K. HINES,
Willow Grove, Pa.

Would Not Take $1,000

I would not take a thousand dollars for what I have learned and it has cost me only a small sum.
MRS. SUSIE M. BOULTON,
La Junta, Colo.

Saves $250

I have just finished counting up how much I have saved since I took up the Dressmaking Course and it has been every cent of $250.00.
MRS. CARL CORBIN,
Urbana, Ill.

Friends Decide to Save, Too

I wouldn't take $500.00 for what this wonderful course has taught me. Many of my friends who knew I couldn't sew were so surprised at the quick results and the pretty things I made that five of them have taken up the same course.
MISS JANET O'NEILL,
Dayton, Ohio

IF you have gone through this book carefully, you must be satisfied that through the Woman's Institute you really can learn, in a surprisingly short time, to make the lovely, attractive, becoming clothes you have wanted.

But there is one last thought we want to leave with you before you lay down this book, and that is the *investment* value of this course. There is no other way in which a small sum of money can bring you back so much in savings and earnings.

If you make only your own and your children's clothes, you can surely save the entire cost of your course the very first year—you may save it twice over. But that is only the beginning. Next year your savings will be as much or more, the next they will be even greater, and so on year after year. The ability to make lovely clothes is something that no one can take from you. It will be yours to use the rest of your life. You pay but a small sum for your training and pay it but once—yet that sum will come back to you again and again and again in savings on your clothes.

If you intend to sew for others, then your profits on this small investment will be even larger. Within a few weeks after starting you can be earning money, in a few weeks more you can have your course entirely paid for, and from that time on you can have a splendid income the rest of your life. So your venture will be doubly profitable. You can not only save half or more on the cost of your own clothes but earn several hundred or possibly several thousand dollars each year through your work for others.

There is no other way in which a woman or girl can, by putting in so small a sum of money, save or earn so much. There are few, if any other investments that will bring back so much happiness, so much genuine helpfulness and satisfaction. Out of years of experience and contact with thousands of our students, we can say with confidence that this will be the best investment you have ever made.

Considered from every angle, joining the Woman's Institute and learning to make the smart distinctive clothes you have always wanted will be the cheapest, the most economical, the wisest thing you can do.

Originally published in "How You Can Have More and Prettier Clothes" Book, 1925

Vintage Notions Monthly continues to share the work of Mary Brooks Picken and the Woman's Institute which inspired my book *Vintage Notions*. Although the Institute was founded 100 years ago, the treasure trove of lessons and stories are still relevant today and offer a blueprint for living a contented life.

If you enjoyed this issue of *Vintage Notions Monthly*, visit AmyBarickman.com for more of my curated collection of vintage content including patterns and books for needle and thread, inspiring fabric and textiles & free vintage art every Friday. Be sure to tune in to *Vintage Notions* episodes for a guided tour through my collection of sewing and fashion history, as well as modern projects inspired by my extensive library.

www.amybarickman.com

Find free images, inspiration and books for the sewing and needle arts!

www.indygojunction.com

Featuring digital & print patterns, books, tutorials, giveaways, project ideas, & more!

Subscribe to each of our eNewsletters to learn about new products, receive special offers, discounts, videos, and get a FREE eBook!

Vintage Notions Monthly , Volume 1, Issue 4 (VN0104)

For wholesale ordering information contact Amy Barickman, LLC at 913.341.5559 or amyb@amybarickman.com, P.O. Box 30238, Kansas City, MO 64112

9 780692 671610